The Fastest C!

Philip Ridley was born ...
he still lives and works. He studied pa...
School of Art. Besides his stage plays, he has direc..
films from his own screenplays: *The Reflecting Skin* (winner of
eleven international awards), *The Passion of Darkly Noon* (winner
of the Best Director Prize at the Porto Film Festival) and
Heartless, starring Jim Sturgess and Timothy Spall. He has also
written five plays for young people: *Karamazoo*, *Fairytaleheart*,
Sparkleshark, *Moonfleece* and *Brokenville*. His many novels for
children include *Scribbleboy* (shortlisted for the Carnegie
Medal), *Kasper in the Glitter* (nominated for the Whitbread
Prize), *Mighty Fizz Chilla* (shortlisted for the *Blue Peter* Book of
the Year Award), *ZinderZunder, Vinegar Street, Zip's Apollo* and
Krindlekrax (winner of both Smarties Prize and WH Smith's
Mind-Boggling Award). His stage adaptation of *Krindlekrax*
premiered at the Birmingham Rep Theatre in 2002. He has
won both the *Evening Standard's* Most Promising Newcomer
to British Film and Most Promising Playwright awards.

Philip Ridley

The Fastest Clock in the Universe

Methuen Drama

Published by Methuen Drama 2009

1 3 5 7 9 10 8 6 4 2

Methuen Drama
A & C Black Publishers Limited
36 Soho Square
London W1D 3QY
www.methuendrama.com

First published in 1992 by Methuen Publishing Ltd.
Revised edition published by Faber and Faber in 1997
in *Philip Ridley Plays 1*
Revised for this edition 2009

A CIP catalogue record for this book is available
from the British Library

ISBN: 978 1 408 12671 4

Typeset by Country Setting, Kingsdown, Kent
Printed and bound in Great Britain by
Cox & Wyman Ltd, Reading, Berkshire

Caution

The Fastest Clock in the Universe

For Dominic Vianney Murphy –
who wears the moon on his skin

Your ideas are shocking and your hearts are faint.
Your acts of pity and cruelty are absurd,
committed casually, as if they were irresistible.
Finally, you fear blood more and more.
Blood and time.

Paul Valéry

There is nothing to be said for you. Guard
Your secret. Conceal it under your hard
plumage, necromancer.

Marianne Moore

I have felt the wind of the wing of madness.

Charles Baudelaire

The Fastest Clock in the Universe premiered at the Hampstead Theatre, London on 14 May 1992, with the following cast:

Cougar Glass   Con O'Neill
Captain Tock   Jonathan Coy
Foxtrot Darling   Jude Law
Sherbet Gravel   Emma Amos
Cheetah Bee   Elizabeth Bradley

Director Matthew Lloyd
Designer Moggie Douglas
Lighting Michael Calf
Sound John A. Leonard

This major revival opened at the Hampstead Theatre, London, on 17 September 2009, with the following cast:

Cougar Glass   Alec Newman
Captain Tock   Finbar Lynch
Foxtrot Darling   Neet Mohan
Sherbet Gravel   Jaime Winstone
Cheetah Bee   Eileen Page

Director Edward Dick
Designer Mark Thompson
Lighting Rick Fisher
Sound Adrienne Quartly

Characters

Cougar Glass
Captain Tock
Foxtrot Darling
Sherbet Gravel
Cheetah Bee

Act One

A dilapidated room above an abandoned factory in the East End of London. Many large cracks in walls. Table, hard-backed chairs, sofa, cupboard, sideboard, window (aglow with setting late-September sunlight), fridge, sink, gas cooker, mirror. The main feature, however, is birds – stuffed birds, china birds, paintings of birds, etc. – giving the room an atmosphere somewhere between museum and aviary. Two doors: the first leading to a bedroom, the second – the front door – to a corridor outside (there is a door at the end of this corridor and a wooden staircase leading down, presumably to the street).

Cougar Glass *is sitting in front of a sun-ray lamp, wearing only his (very sexy and stylish) underpants and sunglasses. He is a young-looking thirty-year-old, suntanned, well-built, hair jet black and roughly styled in a quiff. In one hand he holds a cigarette, in the other a bottle of beer.*

Cougar *sips beer, then puffs cigarette.*

Pause.

Footsteps approach down corridor. The front door opens.

Captain Tock *enters. He is forty-nine years old, pale, slightly built and severely balding. He is wearing a button-up white shirt (without tie) and suit. He is holding a gold-coloured cake box.*

Captain *closes door.*

Captain I've just had a shocking experience.

Cougar *doesn't react.*

Slight pause.

Remember that bird I've been telling you about? The one under the bridge. Down Brick Lane? Caught in some wire or something?

Slight pause.

All last week it was flapping its wings. And – good Lord! – the squalling! Quite deafening. You know how everything echoes under that bridge.

Slight pause.

It was a magpie.

Slight pause.

Are you listening, Cougar?

Cougar *flicks ash on the floor.*

Captain   Oh, what a petty thing to do.

Puts cake box down and gets dustpan and brush.

What d'you think I am? Your skivvy?

Gets to his knees and sweeps up ash.

I've got better things to do with my time.

Cougar *flicks ash on* **Captain**'s *head.*

Captain   Oh, good Lord! Really, Cougar! Really! This kind of behaviour is just uncalled for.

Brushes himself and stands.

I've got to get things ready for your party. So don't try my patience.

Puts dustpan and brush away.

That sun-ray lamp must be eating half your brain away. The half with consideration. I'll get you an ashtray.

He puts ashtray near **Cougar**.

Cougar *stabs out cigarette.*

Captain   I suppose you want another cigarette now?

Cougar *grins.*

Captain *puts cigarette in* **Cougar**'s *mouth and lights it.*

Captain   I adore it when you breathe deeply. Your stomach muscles tensing. Like rows of packed walnuts.

Cougar *finishes his beer, then slams empty bottle on table.*

Captain   Another drink now, is it?

Cougar *grins.*

Captain *gets bottle of beer from fridge, opens it, then hands it to*
Cougar.

Captain *disposes of empty bottle.*

Captain   I'm not drinking any alcohol tonight, Cougar.
Party or no party. And I'm not eating any of that birthday
cake either. It's no good me taking all my vitamins, then filling
my stomach with rubbish. It wears away my defences. And
what would you do if anything happened to me? You wouldn't
find anyone else to wait on you hand and foot. Do you want
anything else?

Cougar *shakes head.*

Captain *approaches* **Cougar**.

Captain   You sure?

Cougar *nods.*

Captain *touches* **Cougar***'s hair.*

Cougar *slaps* **Captain***'s hand away.*

Captain   Aha! Now I've got your attention, I'll tell you
about the magpie. Under the bridge. Down Brick Lane. The
bird I've been telling you about. Remember? Well, children
have been throwing things at it, of course. 'Leave the bird
alone,' I've been telling them. 'Let it die in peace.' Would they
listen? Course not. And every day the bird got thinner and
thinner. And the squalls got fainter and fainter. It must have
been so beautiful once. And now it was just target practice for
brutal children. When it finally died, I heaved a sigh of relief.
It won't suffer any more, I thought. But it started to rot. The
legs caught in the wire started to wither away.

Cougar *winces.*

Captain   Don't worry. I'll spare you the gruesome details.
I knew that – one day – the bird was going to fall. So every

morning and every evening, as I walked under the bridge, I
kept one eye on where I was going and one eye on that bird.
Watching for the telltale signs of disintegrating legs. But this
evening . . . this evening I didn't watch. And you know why?
Because I had your birthday cake in my hands. So I had both
my eyes on the pavement in case I slipped in some moist bird
droppings. And, naturally, tonight the bird fell. It missed me,
I'm glad to say. But only by a few inches. Of course, in a way,
I count myself lucky. It could have landed on my head. What
would that have looked like? Me walking home with a rotten
magpie on my head.

Captain *touches* **Cougar***'s hair.*

Hands mirror to **Cougar***.*

Captain   It's an omen. I know it. One for sorrow. That's
what the old nursery rhyme says about magpies, doesn't it?
One for sorrow. Remember? How does the rest go? Two for
joy. Yes. That's it. Then three for a . . . oh, what is it? Three
for a . . . girl. Yes. A girl. And four for a . . . What was four
for, Cougar? Do you remember? What was four for?

Slight pause.

What was four for, Cougar? Four for a –

Cougar   Boy.

Captain   Hallelujah! I knew you were listening. A boy! Of
course. A boy. Then five for silver, six for gold and seven . . .
Seven, Cougar? What was seven for? Seven for a . . . ?

Cougar   Secret.

Captain   That's right! Seven for a secret never to be told.
Thank you, Cougar. That was a great help. Then eight was a
wish, and nine was a kiss.

He touches **Cougar***'s hair.*

Cougar *slaps* **Captain***'s hand.*

Captain   All right, all right! I can tell when you're getting
irritated. That little pucker appears on your brow.

Cougar   Wrinkle?

Captain   No, Cougar. Not a wrinkle. A pucker. There's a difference.

Cougar   Mirror!

Captain   Good Lord! Shall I get the dictionary? You see, a pucker is –

Cougar   Mirror!

Captain *gets hand mirror.*

Captain   If you don't want wrinkles, you should stay away from that lamp. You know what sunlight does to you. It dries you out. Turns you into a wrinkled old prune before your time.

Hands mirror to **Cougar**.

Cougar *takes sunglasses off and studies his reflection.*

Captain   I wish I could look into the mirror with your confidence. Inspect my face with such interest and find only delight. Mirrors have never been kind to me. I even approach shop windows with caution in case my reflection leaps into view. You see, I have this image in my mind of what I look like. But for some reason, it doesn't correspond with what mirrors tell me. It must be glorious to know your appearance is a source of wonder. No matter where you go people are content merely to gaze at you. That has always eluded me. I can't even say I was beautiful once.

Cougar   You had hair once.

Captain   Was I beautiful when I had hair?

Cougar   No.

Captain   Your honesty is crippling. And, by the way, you've missed a few.

Cougar   Missed a few?

Captain   Grey hairs. Round the back.

Cougar *strains to see with mirror.*

Cougar   I can't see.

Captain   Well, they're there.

Cougar   I left the dye on for two hours. Even did my eyebrows.

Captain   The eyebrows are fine. It's just the grey hairs round the back that give the game away.

Cougar   Get the tweezers, Captain.

Captain   I'm busy getting the party ready. What time's your guest arriving?

Cougar   Same as usual.

Captain   Then we haven't got long.

Checks wristwatch.

Good Lord, stopped again.

Looks at mantelpiece.

Where's the − ? Cougar? Where's the clock? And the one over there?

Cougar   I smashed them.

Captain   What?

Cougar   Warned you I would.

Captain   Why? Why?

Goes to waste bin.

Cougar   They deserved to be smashed! Fucking clocks! Nothing to do but to sit there ticking!

Captain *gets remains of clocks from waste bin.*

Captain   They were mine. From the antique shop.

Cougar   Oh, your *junk* shop!

Captain   Antique shop!

Cougar   You sell people's old crap!

Captain   Antiques!

Cougar   Junk clocks from a junk shop!

Captain   Well, at least we could tell the bloody time!

Pause.

Cougar   You going to get the tweezers or what? I can't have a nineteenth birthday party with my hair turning grey.

Slight pause.

Captain *goes to cupboard, gets tweezers, approaches* **Cougar**.

Captain   Turn that lamp off, then. You know how delicate my skin is.

Cougar   You turn it off. I'm cooking nicely.

Captain *turns sun-ray lamp off, then stands behind* **Cougar**, *searching for grey hairs.*

Captain   Your selfishness is awesome. You don't put yourself out for anyone. You're nothing but a fiend who expects everything –

Cougar   Fiend! Where do you dig all these words up from?

Captain *starts to look for grey hairs but –*

Captain   It's too dark now.

Cougar   Christ Almighty!

Captain   Don't be so irritable all the time.

He goes to main light switch. He flicks it on. The lights flicker on and off violently.

Come on, lights!

The lights continue to flicker.

Cougar   One day this whole fucking building will just . . . crumble away.

The lights stay on.

Captain   There!

He begins searching **Cougar***'s hair again.*

Cougar   Hang on! Show me your fingernails.

Captain   What?

Cougar   Fingernails!

Captain   They're fine, Cougar.

Cougar   Then show me!

Captain *shows* **Cougar** *his fingernails.*

Cougar   Oh, they're revolting, Captain. Christ Almighty! You've been biting them again. I don't know how you can just gnaw and gnaw at them like that. Look! All the skin is chewed away. They might leak at any minute. Put the gloves on.

Captain   But it's hard to get a grip on the tweezers with the –

Cougar   I'm not having you leak all over me, Captain. Gloves!

Captain *gets some pink, rubber washing-up gloves and puts them on.*

Cougar   You know what you should do? Go outside and stick your fingers in some of that bird shit. That'd stop you biting your nails.

Captain *resumes searching for* **Cougar***'s grey hairs.*

Captain   Don't be disgusting.

Cougar   I'm not being disgusting. It's a good idea. There's so much shit everywhere, you might as well put it to use – Oww!

Flinches as hair is plucked.

That hurt!

Captain   Don't fuss.

Cougar   You're doing it on purpose.

Captain   Stop squirming.

Cougar   You're only jealous – Oww! There you go again. What is this? The baldy's revenge?

Captain   Don't, Cougar. Please.

Cougar   You must walk round with a pair of tweezers in your pocket. Then, when you see a man with a healthy head of hair, on a bus or something, or when you're walking through the park, or in your junk shop – sorry! *antique* shop! – you creep up behind them and pluck out a few hairs.

Captain   Stop it, Cougar. It's not funny. It's hurtful.

Cougar   You should set up your own little society. You know, the Bald Phantom Hair Pluckers or something like that. You get together once a month – when the moon is full, or something – and compare how many hairs you've managed to pluck.

Captain   I'm not laughing.

Cougar   Well, I am! It's fucking hilarious! I can imagine it now. When . . . when you become a member you're given – not a comb, but a piece of cloth and some polish and . . . and you all sit there having skin-polishing contests.

Captain *slams tweezers down and walks away.*

Captain   Do it yourself! I can't take it any more. All the little jibes and jokes. Upsetting me for no reason. After I've been running around to get things ready for your birthday party as well. Getting the cake. Everything. And what thanks do I get? None. Well, I've had it up to the back teeth. Hear me? Back teeth . . . I'm going to dust a baby.

He gets a china bird and starts dusting it.

Pause.

Cougar   Captain . . .

Captain   I'm dusting!

Slight pause.

Cougar   I'm sorry, Captain.

Captain   Too late. You think you can just say you're sorry and everything will be forgiven. Well, you've gone too far this time.

Slight pause.

Cougar   Is it over then?

Captain   Yes.

Cougar   No more larks?

Captain   No more larks.

Cougar   You don't mean it.

Captain   I most certainly do.

Cougar   But what will Cougar do without his Captain?

Captain   You should have thought of that earlier.

Cougar   But you know I'm always on pins on my birthday-party nights. You know what I'm like, don't you? You know I'm on pins.

Captain   . . . I know.

Cougar   And you know I've asked you – asked you millions of times, Captain – to make allowances when I'm on pins. But you don't. You just get in a tizz.

Captain   I am not in a tizz.

Cougar   When I'm so happy and everything was going so well. I was looking forward to the party. And afterwards we would have talked and had a hug and I would have said, 'Let's have some larks,' or words to that effect. But you have to spoil it all by getting into a tizz just because I'm on pins.

Pause.

Captain   Cougar . . .

Cougar   Well, if it's over then it's over. If the Captain don't want his Cougar then I best pack my bags and clear off.

Stands.

Captain   I'm sorry, Cougar.

Cougar   No you're not. You're still in a tizz.

Captain   I'm not in a tizz.

Cougar   You know I'm on pins.

Captain   I know. And I am sorry. Don't go. Please sit down. Let me finish plucking your hair.

Cougar   No more palaver?

Captain   No more palaver.

Cougar   Apology accepted.

Sits.

Captain   Can I give you a hug?

Cougar   If you have to.

Captain *approaches* **Cougar**.

Cougar   Put your gloves on, though.

Captain *puts gloves on.*

Cougar   You see, it's all too much for me, Captain. You getting into a tizz. It puts my head in a bloody spin.

Captain *hugs* **Cougar**.

Captain   I'm sorry. It won't happen again.

Cougar   That's enough hugging.

Captain   A moment longer.

Cougar   I'm getting all claustrophobic.

Pushes **Captain** *away.*

Pause.

Cougar   Did you like the hug?

Captain   Very much.

Cougar *hands* **Captain** *tweezers.*

Captain *resumes looking for grey hairs.*

Cougar   Anyway, I ain't the only one.

Captain   Eh? What?

Cougar   Who's had enough.

Captain   Enough of what?

Cougar   The birds in the factory.

Captain   Oh, don't start that again.

Cougar   No, listen, Captain. Cheetah Bee said she's had a gullet full too.

Captain   Cheetah Bee? But she's always been fond of the birds.

Cougar   Not any more. Vermin, she reckons.

Captain   Vermin!?

Cougar   She's had men in.

Captain   What men?

Cougar   Two of them. They were here today. In white overalls. They're going to . . . to . . .

Waits for **Captain** *to supply the word.*

Captain   Exterminate?

Cougar   That's it. *Exterminate* the birds.

Captain   But that's terrible.

Cougar   Why?

Captain   *When* are they going to do it?

Cougar   Fuck knows. But you want to know a very interesting fact?

Captain What?

Cougar I went to school with one of the men. Can you
believe that? I tell you, Captain, time has not been kind to
him. Receding hairline. Skin all pasty and wrinkled. Bags
under his eyes. Double chin. Hairs hanging from his nostrils
and sticking out his ears. And as for his body. Christ Almighty.
Don't know if I can still call it a body. Fat. Shapeless. Round
shoulders. He came up here and he was wheezing like a
geriatric. He said to me, 'Cougar,' he said, 'you look just the
same as the day you were expelled.' I thought, 'Wish I could
say the same for you, old son.' Old being the operative word –
Oww! Thought you said there were only a few.

Captain You want me to get all of them, don't you?

Pause.

Cougar He had his son with him. His son's helping him.
We went over the park.

Captain All three of you?

Cougar Just me and the son.

Captain What did you do?

Cougar Had a banana split.

Captain You shouldn't eat ice cream.

Cougar Not getting fat, am I?

Captain It's not good for your insides.

Cougar Who gives a fuck about my insides? Can have a
gut full of maggots for all I care, so long as I've got a suntan.

Slight pause.

Captain So . . . how old is he?

Cougar Who?

Captain The son.

Cougar Didn't ask.

Captain   Can't be very old if you went to school with his dad.

Cougar   I said, didn't ask.

Captain   . . . Has he got nice hair?

Cougar   Who?

Captain   The son.

Cougar   A little short.

Captain   So you suggested he grow it? Style it into a quiff?

Cougar   How d'you guess?

Captain   And he already thinks you're the most exciting person he's ever met.

Cougar   Don't they all, Captain? – Ahhh! What you trying to do? Scalp me?

Captain   All finished.

Cougar   Took you long enough.

Captain *puts gloves and tweezers away.*

Captain   You best get ready for the party, Cougar.

Cougar *goes to bedroom.*

Captain *puts sunlamp in corner. It flashes violently a few times.*

He puts tablecloth on table.

Cougar (*from bedroom*)   Have we got everything, Captain?

Captain   Everything.

Cougar (*from bedroom*)   The vodka?

Captain   Yes.

Cougar (*from bedroom*)   Because he only drinks vodka.

Captain   I got a bottle.

Cougar (*from bedroom*)   Just one?

Captain   It'll be enough. I'm not going to drink. I told you.

Cougar (*from bedroom*)   What mixer did you get?

Captain   Orange juice.

Cougar (*from bedroom*)   Orange juice?!

Captain   It's what you told me to get!

Cougar *comes out of bedroom. He is wearing a white T-shirt, black leather jacket, faded denim jeans and black-leather boots and sunglasses. His hair is now styled into an impeccable quiff. He is splashing on some aftershave.*

Cougar   Smell me.

Captain   What?

Cougar   Come on. Have a whiff.

Captain *sniffs.*

Captain   Good Lord! It's strong. What is it?

Cougar *shows* **Captain** *the bottle.*

Captain   Expensive stuff. Nice to know my money's being spent wisely.

Cougar *puts bottle on sideboard.*

Cougar   I'm wearing it for a purpose.

Captain   What sort of purpose?

Cougar   On purpose.

Slight pause.

What about the birthday cards?

Captain   Oh . . . yes. Of course.

Captain *gets cards from drawer*

Cougar   You get any new ones?

Captain   No. We can use the ones from last time.

Cougar   How many are there?

Captain   Seven.

Cougar   Who they from again?

Looks in mirror, takes comb from pocket and combs his already perfect hair.

Captain   Tracy, Sonya, Natasha, Sharon, Jade, Lesley and Kylie.

Cougar   All girls?

Captain   That's what we had before. Anyway, Lesley could be a boy.

Cougar   But he'll assume it's a girl. I've told him I've got lots of male friends as well. Everyone likes me. Not just girls. I'm popular, Captain. Popular.

Captain   Well, we haven't got any new cards.

Cougar   You'll have to think of something, Captain. I want to have male friends as well. Hear me? Male friends. Mates! Mates!

Pause.

Captain   Perhaps we should make a few of the cards from both a boy and girl. As if they've been sent by a couple.

Cougar   Knew you'd think of something.

Captain *starts amending cards.*

Captain   Tracy and . . . Russell?

Cougar   Nah. Tracy and Rod.

Captain   Sonya and . . .

Cougar   Robbie.

Captain   Sharon and . . . Peter?

Cougar   Yeah. Peter. Perfect.

Captain   That should be enough. Happy now?

Cougar   Happy now.

Captain *gets cake out of box and puts it on table.*

Cougar   We should still get some more cards just for male friends. Cards from Zack and Marky and Dean and Troy . . . Names like that.

Captain   Come and look at the cake, Cougar.

Cougar *looks at cake.*

Captain   They did us proud this time. Isn't it delectable?

Cougar   If you say so.

Captain   But look at all that icing, Cougar. The white against the blue.

Cougar   Don't know why you're so bothered. You ain't eating any.

Captain   I can still look at it.

Cougar   You're supposed to eat it, Captain. That's why it's made of yummy things and not sawdust.

Captain   I get more enjoyment from looking at it than you get from consuming it.

Cougar   I very much doubt it.

Captain   That's because you have no aesthetics.

Cougar   Fuck aesthetics. Just stick the candles in and hide it in the bedroom. It's supposed to be a surprise. He likes surprises.

Captain   Don't refer to him as he. Say his name.

Cougar   I forget his fucking name.

Captain   Don't be ridiculous.

Cougar   I tell you when he gets here, don't I?

Captain   Tell me now.

Slight pause.

Tell me now!

Cougar   Foxtrot . . .

Captain   Foxtrot what?

Cougar   Foxtrot Darling.

Captain   Oh, what an enchanting name!

Cougar *glares at* **Captain**.

Pause.

Captain   I'll . . . I'll get the candles.

He goes to cupboard, gets candles, then returns to table.

Cougar *continues to glare at* **Captain**.

Captain   How many candles shall I put in, Cougar?

Cougar *just stares.*

Pause.

Captain   All nineteen?

Cougar *just stares.*

Pause.

Captain   You're right. All nineteen. Same as always. After all, it *is* your nineteenth birthday party.

He starts sticking candles into birthday cake.

Pause.

Cougar   I don't need to know his name to do what I'm going to do to him.

Captain   I . . . I know.

Pause.

Cougar   No need for gloves where he's concerned.

Captain   Don't . . . please.

He stops sticking candles in cake. There is one remaining.

Slight pause.

Cougar   Stick the last candle in, then.

Pause.

Stick it in.

Captain *doesn't move.*

Cougar   Stick. It. In.

He takes candle from **Captain**'s *hand and – with a very gentle orgasmic moan – thrusts candle into cake.*

Cougar   Got to do everything myself now, have I?

Captain   I'm sorry.

Cougar   You take things too seriously. That's your problem.

Captain   I take you seriously. I have feelings for you.

Cougar   Then don't. Life's too short to have feelings for people.

Captain   Don't you have feelings for me?

Cougar   I need you, Captain.

Captain   Just need?

Cougar   Now don't get all agitated.

Captain   I'm not getting all agitated. I'm only asking.

Cougar   But you've asked it all before. The same old questions. Over and over again. What good does it do? I need you. Full stop. End of discussion.

Pause.

Captain *picks up cake.*

Captain   I'll hide this so I can surprise you with it later.

He takes cake into bedroom.

Cougar   Larks, Captain! Don't forget we have our larks!

Slight pause.

Captain *enters from bedroom.*

Captain   I can feel one building up.

Cougar   No! Don't!

Captain *moves towards window.*

Cougar *tries to stop him.*

Cougar   You'll just disturb the bloody birds.

Captain   If I don't do it, I'm going to explode.

Cougar   I don't want screaming birds when he gets here.

They struggle together.

Captain   Don't hinder me, Cougar.

Cougar   You know, you're stronger than you look.

Captain   I'll leak on you!

Cougar *backs away.*

Captain *goes to window and opens it. He sticks his head out and screams. The sound of birds squalling begins. It is piercingly loud!*

Cougar   There! You've done it now!

Captain *faces* **Cougar**.

Captain   Good Lord! Listen to them, Cougar!

Cougar   Ain't got no fucking choice, have I?!

Captain   Fly! Fly!

Cougar   They'll be shitting everywhere!

Captain   Oh, to fly with them, Cougar! To fly and make sounds like that!

He starts to move round room, flapping his arms.

Cougar *laughs.*

Captain   To fly through the clouds –

Cougar (*overlapping*)   One of these days –

Captain (*overlapping*)   – and scream and scream –

Cougar (*overlapping*)   – men in white coats –

Captain (*overlapping*)   – and not belong to anything –

Cougar (*overlapping*)   – will come and take you away.

Captain (*overlapping*)   – or anyone –

Cougar (*overlapping*)   They'll put you in a funny farm.

Captain (*overlapping*)   – and just be free. Free!

Cougar   Not much fucking freedom there.

Captain   Fly! Fly! Fly!

Cougar *shuts window and pulls curtain.*

Captain *collapses on sofa, giddy.*

Cougar   You'll make yourself sick, you will.

The birds are getting quieter.

Captain   They're calming now! Back to your nests!

Cougar   I'll give you back to your fucking nests. What if they'd carried on like that all bloody night? What kind of party would I have had then? . . . Christ Almighty.

Laughs and sits next to **Captain**

Cougar   You're a silly old sod sometimes, Captain. Really you are.

They lean against each, laughing.

The sound of the birds gradually fades.

Pause.

Captain   I have . . . I have this memory, Cougar. Of what it was like. Perhaps it was only for a week. Or day. Near the beginning of . . . us. A moment when you gave me something. Remember that, Cougar? The Fastest Clock in the Universe. You gave it to me once. Will you ever give it to me again?

Long pause.

Something strikes the window from outside.

Captain   Good Lord!

Cougar   Christ Almighty!

Captain *stands.*

Captain   It's a bird, Cougar!

Cougar   Forget it.

Captain *walks toward window.*

Cougar   Leave it.

Captain   It might be injured.

Cougar   There's fuck-all we can do.

Captain   We can nurse it.

Cougar   Leave it, Captain! Come on. Let's choose a magazine for the party. You know how it makes you giggle.

Opens cupboard.

It is full of pornographic magazines.

Cougar   Come and help me, Captain.

Captain   I shouldn't have screamed.

Cougar   Look at the pictures. You know they make you giggle. Come on.

Captain *peers out of the window.*

Captain   It's on the window ledge, Cougar.

Cougar   Have a fucking giggle, Captain!

Pause.

Captain *faces* **Cougar**.

Captain   What?

Cougar *holds magazine in air.*

Cougar   Giggle!

Captain   Good Lord! Yes, I'm sorry, Cougar.

Slowly **Captain** *goes over to* **Cougar**.

They spread magazines on floor and start sorting through them.

Captain   What does . . . Foxtrot like?

Cougar   Women with women.

Captain   Lesbians.

Cougar   Oh, don't get all technical.

Captain   I'm not getting all tech –

Cougar   Find me a good one, Captain. Lots of tongues up pussies and stuff . . . Christ Almighty! Some of these magazines go back to when I was twelve. That's how old I was when I got my first magazine. Me and my best friend stole it. We went to the block of flats where my mate lived and rushed up to the roof. We sat amongst the television aerials and looked at the photographs. I had an erection so hard it hurt. I persuaded my mate to get his cock out. I got mine out too. We played with each other. And then . . . then I got this feeling somewhere in my gut. Like a tiny explosion. And I spunked. It was my first ejaculation. I never dreamed a body could feel something like that. Christ Almighty! I'll never forget it. Sitting up there. Amongst all those television aerials. Somehow, I felt like I was part of an electric current. Every nerve in my body was transmitting particles of sex. My brain sparkled. My hair stood on end. Blood simmered. I imagined myself glowing. A halo of lust buzzing round me. The first real moment of my fucking life.

Pause.

Captain *hands* **Cougar** *magazine.*

Captain   Tongues up pussies.

Cougar *looks at magazine.*

Cougar   Perfect.

He goes to sofa.

Cougar   Put the magazines away, Captain.

Captain *starts to put magazines back in cupboard.*

Cougar *hides magazine under sofa, then sits on sofa and practises reaching below to produce magazine from under sofa in one swift movement.*

Captain *begins flicking through a magazine.*

Captain   I don't know what it is about the sight of skin that makes me weep.

Cougar *looks at* **Captain**.

Pause.

Cougar   Come on, slowcoach. We've got to get things ready.

Captain   Oh . . . yes. Of course.

Puts remaining magazines in cupboard.

Cougar   Now, you know what to do, don't you, Captain?

Captain   Same as all the other parties, I suppose.

Cougar   We'll let him in.

Captain   I know, Cougar. I know.

Cougar   Have a few drinks.

Captain   That's why I bought the vodka.

Cougar   Tell him how popular I am.

Captain   Thousands of girlfriends.

Cougar   They follow me everywhere.

Captain   Like flies.

Cougar   And all the time you're . . . ?

Captain   Pouring vodka.

Cougar   Not too much. Don't want him to pass out.

Captain   Just tipsy.

Cougar   Then I'll give you the signal to leave.

Captain   And I'll go. Farewell, Foxtrot Darling.

Cougar   And the signal is?

Captain   What?

Cougar   What's the signal for you to leave the party?

Captain   Good Lord! What's this? A test now?

Cougar   Just tell me, Captain. I don't want any cock-ups tonight.

Captain   I thought that's precisely what you wanted.

Cougar   Eh?

Captain   . . . Oh, never mind.

Cougar   Just tell me the signal for you to leave the party, for chrissakes.

Captain   You'll say, 'Isn't it time for your meeting, Captain?'

Cougar   And you'll say?

Captain   'Good Lord, yes, Cougar! Thank you for reminding me!'

Cougar   And you'll disappear.

Captain   I'll have to walk the streets again, I suppose.

Cougar   By the time you get back, he'll be gone.

Captain   And you'll never want to see him again.

Cougar   Why the fuck would I want to see him again?

Captain *stares at* **Cougar**.

Captain   Oh, Cougar.

Pause.

Cougar   I ain't told you how I met him yet. And you've got to know, Captain. There's a . . . an *extra* bit this time.

Captain   What '*extra*' bit?

Cougar   A sort of . . . trap.

Captain *starts putting knives, forks, plates, glasses, etc. on table.*

Captain   Trap? Good Lord! What now?

Cougar   Listen. I was sunbathing in the park when . . . there he was. Walking very fast and holding some flowers. I was going to follow him, but I couldn't get my boots on quick enough. You would have laughed.

Slight pause.

Next day. I'm sunbathing again when – hello, hello. There he is! Walking just as fast as before and – again – he's holding some flowers. But again – fuck! – I couldn't get my bloody boots on in time. So the following day, guess what I did?

Captain   I'm all ears.

Cougar   Didn't take my boots off! Ha! Good thinking, eh, Captain? This time I thought, when I see him, I'll be ready – There! Him! Follow! Oh, Captain, I really like the way he walks. His arse is so . . .

Captain   All right, all right.

Cougar   Then I saw where he was heading. The London-fucking-hospital.

Captain   Aha! The flowers.

Cougar   Exactly. I followed him inside.

Captain   But you hate hospitals.

Cougar   Shows how much I wanted him, don't it? He went into a ward. I was gonna follow him in there too but – oh, just the thought of all those sick people. Made me wanna puke. I waited outside. Seemed like fucking hours. I walked up and down – There! He's coming out of the ward – Hang on! What's that on his arm? It's a fucking girl!

Captain   Oh, dear.

Cougar   I wanted to smash her fucking face in!

Captain   Temper, temper.

Cougar   I couldn't help it. He was so . . . perfect. That slag didn't deserve him. I piss off out the hospital. I'm shaking, Captain. Shaking. That night I couldn't stop thinking about him. He was gnawing at me and gnawing at me – Oh, the table's coming along nicely, Captain.

Captain   I'm doing my best.

Cougar   I went back, you know.

Captain   What? Not *into* the hospital?

Cougar   The very next day.

Captain   Good Lord.

Cougar   I was outside the ward when he turned up. He caught my eye as he went in. I do this sad little smile I'd been practising. I wait. I get a cup of tea from the machine thing. I drink it – There he is! No girl.

Your moment to pounce.

Cougar   'Hello, mate. What you looking all sad for?'

Captain   Who was he visiting?

Cougar   His dying brother.

Captain   What was he dying of?

Cougar   Oh, something terminal. And the girl, Captain – that fucking floozie on his arm – she wasn't *his* girlfriend at all. She was his *brother's* girlfriend. Yesss! And then . . . then a plan started taking shape in my brain. The perfect trap.

Captain *has finished setting the table.*

Captain   There! All finished!

Cougar   Sit down, Captain.

Captain   How does it look?

Cougar   Fine. Just sit down.

Captain   You could show a little appreciation.

Cougar   I said it looks fucking fine. What more d'you want?
A medal? Now sit the fuck down.

Pause.

Captain *sits.*

Cougar   I've got to tell you about the trap.

Slight pause.

Captain   So? What is it?

Cougar   Not *what*, Captain. *Who?*

Captain   *Who*, then?

Cougar   . . . Savannah Glass.

Captain   Savannah Glass?

Cougar   My wife.

Captain   Your *what?*

Cougar   My dying wife. My poor dying wife who – wait for
it! – just happened to be in the same hospital as his poor
dying brother.

Captain   Oh, no, Cougar.

Cougar   What's wrong?

Captain   I know you're not exactly the milk of human
kindness, but not even you can be so cruel.

Cougar   Don't make a song and dance out of it.

Captain   To play with the boy's feelings like that. To
manipulate him so callously.

Cougar   But it's such a perfect lie, Captain. I had to think of
something to keep meeting him at the hospital, didn't I? Eh?
And it meant I didn't have to say hello to the dying brother's
floozie. 'Oh, I'm too upset to meet girls. You understand, don't

you, mate?' And me and him – we became united in our grief.
Oh, come on. Credit where credit's due.

Captain   It's toying with someone's grief!

Cougar   Exactly!

Captain   But it's monstrous! To simply *invent* a wife for
yourself – worse! to invent a *dying* wife! – just so you can . . .
can have your way with that poor, grieving –

Cougar   I comforted him, Captain! Put my arm round him.
Said I understood when he needed someone to understand.
We suffered together. Sometimes he cried when I held him.
Have you any idea what a buzz that is? And guess what,
Captain. His brother and my wife – what a coincidence! –
they died on exactly the same day.

Captain *stands.*

Captain   I won't be part of it.

Cougar   You're already bloody part of it!

Captain   I'm not. I'll go before Foxtrot gets here. It's too
much, Cougar. Even for you. It's too heartless.

Cougar   Oh, boo-hoo.

Captain   It's diabolical!

Cougar   Spoilsport!

Captain   Cannibal!

Cougar   Cannibal?!

Captain   Yes! Cannibal!

Cougar   Christ Almighty! The words you come up with.

Captain   To treat the boy like that is just –

Cougar   He's not a boy.

Captain   How old is he?

Cougar   Didn't ask.

Captain   How bloody old? Tell me! . . . Tell me!

Cougar   Fifteen.

Captain   What?

Cougar   You heard!

Captain   He's a boy, Cougar! A child!

Cougar   He's not. He can get a hard-on. He can spunk. He's a man, for fuck's sake. A man!

Captain   He's a child and you've used him abominably.

Cougar   I gave him what he wanted. A new big brother with a shoulder to cry on. So don't get all righteous with me. We're all as bad as each other. All hungry little cannibals at our own cannibal party. So fuck the milk of human kindness and welcome to the abattoir!

Pause.

Captain   It's about time you bloody grew up.

Cougar   Careful, Captain.

Captain   All these endless nineteenth birthday parties.

Cougar   You'll say something you'll regret.

Captain   You can't be a teenager all your life.

Cougar   Don't say it!

Captain   You've got to accept your age.

Cougar *starts clutching at his head in pain.*

Cougar   Don't. Don't, Captain.

Continues to clutch at his head.

Captain   . . . Cougar?

Cougar   It's hurting, Captain!

Captain   But . . . but I didn't actually *say* your age.

Cougar   Hurting!

Captain   Keep in control. Don't get violent. Please. Listen to me. I did not say your age.

Slight pause.

Shall I get you a drink?

Cougar   No.

Captain   A cigarette? Would that help?

Cougar   Get Cheetah Bee.

Captain   Cheetah Bee? Oh, it can't be as bad as that, surely!

Cougar   Get her! Quick!

Falls to his knees. He is whimpering. His sunglasses fall off.

Captain *rushes out of room and down corridor.*

Captain   Cheetah Bee! Cheetah Bee!

Knocks on door at end of corridor.

Cheetah Bee! It's the Captain!

Cheetah Bee *opens door. She is eighty-eight years old, very wrinkled and virtually toothless. She is wearing a long brown fur coat and walks with the aid of a walking-frame.*

Cheetah   What's all the hubbub?

Captain   Forgive me, Cheetah Bee. But I'm afraid it's Cougar.

Cheetah   Oh, not again, Captain.

Starts to make her way down corridor.

Captain *hovers beside her, edging her on.*

Cheetah   Don't pull me, Captain.

Captain   I'm sorry.

Cheetah   I can only go so fast, you know.

Captain   Of course you can. It's just that it's a special night for Cougar.

Cheetah   Another party?

Captain   Another party.

Captain *and* **Cheetah Bee** *enter room and approach* **Cougar**.

Captain   Just look at him, Cheetah Bee. What did I tell you?

Cougar*'s whimpering is getting louder.*

Cheetah *stands in front of* **Cougar**.

Slight pause.

Cheetah   Look at me, young man!

Cougar *goes quiet but does not look up.*

Slight pause.

Cheetah   Look at me, I said!

Slowly, **Cougar** *looks.*

Cheetah   Look at my skin. It is wrinkled and pale. Your skin is tanned and smooth. Why? Because I am at the end and you are at the beginning. Look at my hair. It is colourless and thin. Your hair is black and thick. Why? Because I am at the end and you are at the beginning.

Cougar *begins to calm down.*

Captain   It's working again.

Cheetah   It always does.

Captain   Carry on. Please. 'Look at my eyes.'

Cheetah   Look at my eyes! My vision is fading. Eyes bloodshot and plagued by cataracts. I've stopped producing tears to ease the pain. Whereas your vision is faultless, eyes clear and bright, watering at will. Why? Because I am at the end and you are at the beginning.

Captain (*in unison with* **Cheetah**)   Because she is at the end and you are at the beginning.

Cheetah   And my teeth! What few I have are brown and rotten. I can only suck my food and my breath smells of decay. Whereas you have a full head of strong, white teeth and your breath is odourless, inviting kisses. Why? Because I am at the end and you are at the beginning.

Captain (*in unison with* **Cheetah**)   Because she is at the end and you are at the beginning.

Cheetah   Everything about me is ruined and faded. I cannot hear properly, walk properly, and all I have before me is sickness and death. But you, everything about you, my stripling, is youthful and perfect. Your hearing is impeccable. You have the agility of an athlete. And you have nothing ahead of you but time, time, time. And why? Because I am at the end and you are at the beginning. I am at the end and you are at the beginning.

Captain (*in unison*)   Because she is at the end and you are at the beginning. Because she is at the end and you are at the beginning.

Cougar *is calm now.*

Captain   Another success, Cheetah Bee.

Cheetah   Sweet Jesus!

Cheetah *sits.*

Captain   Come and sit down, Cougar.

Captain *helps* **Cougar** *to sofa.*

Cheetah   Hungry work.

Captain   What? Oh . . . yes. Of course. Can I get you something? For all your trouble.

Cheetah   That's very generous of you. I am about to cook my tea.

Captain   What might tickle your fancy?

Cheetah   Have you got any red meat?

Captain   I believe I have.

Goes to fridge.

Gets some liver wrapped in silver foil and takes it to **Cheetah**.

Captain   Liver.

Cheetah   Ah, liver is it?! In that case I shall make my very special gravy. I make it with vinegar and flour. Very thick and tangy. Let me see . . .

Opens silver foil.

Cougar *moans, nauseous.*

Captain   Why don't you lie down for a while, Cougar? You want to be well for your guest. He should be here any minute now.

Leads **Cougar** *to bedroom.*

Captain   It's the liver, Cheetah Bee. He's got such a weak stomach.

Captain *and* **Cougar** *go into bedroom.*

Cheetah   He's too squeamish, that's his trouble. Squeamish is the last thing you can be when you watch as much television as I do. They're apt to surprise you with a documentary on amputees at any minute.

Captain *enters from bedroom.*

Cheetah   Captain, he turns into a wild animal when you say his age. You should have learnt your lesson by now.

Captain   But I didn't say it.

Cheetah   Then you threatened to.

Slight pause.

I don't want any more violence.

Captain   There won't be any more violence.

Pause.

Cougar told me you had the exterminators in. For the birds.

Cheetah   Oh, it has to be done. There's too many of them
now.

Captain   But you always said you were so fond of –

Cheetah   Their shit's rotting everything! . . . It's hard to
believe how beautiful this building once was. 'Immaculate
Fur'. It was written in gold outside. The most famous furriers
in East London. My husband – God rest his soul – no one
knew fur like him. He lived fur. He breathed fur. We provided
fur for film stars.

Captain   Remarkable, yes.

Cheetah   After we married and I'd moved into our little flat
above the factory, he gave me this.

Indicates her fur coat.

The luckiest girl in the world. That's what I thought I was.
I was considered a beauty, Captain.

Captain   I don't doubt it.

Cheetah   'But you must never go down to the factory.'
That's what my husband said to me. 'I give you this gift, but
you must never see how the gift is made.' I understood, of
course. 'Promise me!' said my husband. I did promise. And,
for a long time, I kept my promise. But then, one day, curiosity
got the better of me and I went downstairs to see how the
animals were killed.

Slight pause.

Captain   And . . . how were they killed?

Cougar (*from bedroom*)   Captain!

Captain   He's calling.

Goes into bedroom.

Pause.

Captain *comes out of bedroom.*

Captain   He wants his sunglasses!

Cheetah   Sweet Jesus!

Captain   And the mirror!

Cheetah   Hallelujah!

Captain *starts to collect things together.*

Captain   He's on the mend, Cheetah Bee, and it's all thanks to you.

Goes into bedroom.

Slight pause.

Foxtrot Darling *comes up stairs at end of corridor. He is fifteen years old, hair black and styled in a quiff, with fragile good looks. He is wearing a school uniform and holding a birthday present wrapped in shiny blue wrapping paper.*

Foxtrot *walks down corridor and nervously enters room.*

Foxtrot   Hello. Am I on time?

Cheetah   Who are you?

Foxtrot   Foxtrot Darling. Am I in the right place?

Cheetah   Have you got a quiff?

Foxtrot   Yeah.

Cheetah   Then you're in the right place.

Foxtrot   Oh, good. I've brought a present. Is that your present?

Cheetah   Where?

Foxtrot   In your lap.

Cheetah   No. It's red meat.

Foxtrot   You're kidding. Are you cooking at the party?

Cheetah   I'm not invited to the party.

Foxtrot Oh, God. I'm sorry. I thought . . . only . . . Is Cougar here?

Cheetah He's in there. With the Captain. They'll both be out in a tick.

Foxtrot I ain't met the Captain yet. I've heard a lot about him, though. Captain Tock. Captain Tock out in a tick – ha, ha!

Cheetah *stares.*

Pause.

Captain *comes out of bedroom.*

Captain He's going to be just fine, Cheetah Bee.

Sees **Foxtrot.**

Captain Good Lord!

Foxtrot I ain't early, am I?

Captain Foxtrot.

Foxtrot That's right, Captain.

Captain Good Lord!

Cheetah *stands.*

Cheetah Time I was going.

Walks towards door.

There's a programme on television tonight. About a boy born in a jungle. Some place. Some time. Born without a face. He's adopted by a surgeon who performs endless operations on him. Gradually, the boy gets a nose, a mouth, ears, eyes. Now he can go to school and do all the things other children do: inject himself with chemicals, watch pornography, arm himself with razor blades, get drunk, get old, wither, die. Sometimes I wonder if it's worth having a face at all.

Heads back to her flat.

Captain *closes door behind her.*

Captain   That was –

Foxtrot   Cheetah Bee. Your landlady. Eighty-eight years old. Her husband owned the old factory below. And now it's full of birds.

Captain   We were just talking about that very thing.

Foxtrot   And all the knick-knacks in this room are yours.

Captain   They're antiques!

Foxtrot   Oh, God! Sorry. Antiques. All these antiques are yours. You get them from the junk shop where you –

Captain   Antique shop!

Foxtrot   Sorry. Antique shop.

Slight pause.

You've been collecting these birds for years.

Captain   Since before you were born.

Foxtrot   You call them your babies.

Captain   And so they are. My babies.

Foxtrot   And dust them all once a day.

Captain   Good Lord! Is there anything you don't know?

Foxtrot   Don't think so. I feel as if I'm part of this world already. Cougar was right. It is like living inside a huge cracked egg.

Captain   I said that. They're my words, not Cougar's.

Pause.

Foxtrot   He ain't ill, is he?

Captain   No. He's combing his hair.

Foxtrot   I've had my hair done the way Cougar likes it.

Captain   So I see.

Foxtrot   D'you think he'll be pleased?

Captain   He'll be over the moon.

Foxtrot   Do I look okay?

Captain   It suits you.

Foxtrot   In my uniform, I mean. Weren't time to change.

Captain   You look absolutely fine.

Foxtrot   Am I the first one here?

Captain   The first and only.

Foxtrot   You're kidding! Oh, God . . . Just me?! I didn't realise it would just be me . . . I hope I ain't made a mistake . . .

Captain   Mistake?

Foxtrot *goes to sit on sofa. Then stops –*

Foxtrot   I was going to sit down. Is that all right? It's rude to do it without being asked or something, ain't it?

Captain   No, please. Sit.

Foxtrot *sits.*

Foxtrot   Don't want to do anything to upset Cougar, you see.

Captain   Of course.

Foxtrot   It's just that . . . well, he did say tonight would be the end of our grieving.

Slight pause.

Did he tell you about . . . about my brother?

Captain   Yes. I'm so very sorry.

Foxtrot   Did Cougar tell you today would have been my brother's birthday as well?

Captain   No. He omitted that one.

Foxtrot   Cougar says a coincidence like that must mean something.

Captain Oh, it means something all right.

Foxtrot Me and him meeting like we did – it's like fate, Cougar said.

Captain Like the planets lining up.

Foxtrot That's what Cougar said. The planets lining up. So both of us could help each other with . . . with what we were going through. Me with my brother. And Cougar with his wife, Savannah . . . He really loved your sister, didn't he?

Slight pause.

Captain I'll just let Cougar know you're here.

Foxtrot Don't rush him on my account. Tell him to take his time.

Captain *goes into bedroom.*

Muffled voices are heard in heated argument.

Captain *comes out of bedroom.*

Foxtrot Nothing wrong, is there?

Captain Nothing at all.

Foxtrot You didn't mention my hair, did you? I want it to be a surprise.

Captain No.

Pause.

Foxtrot My brother used to take ages getting ready, too.

Captain He did?

Foxtrot Oh, yeah. Combing his hair. Ironing his shirt. Putting on aftershave. I wanted to be like him so much. Does that sound stupid? Suppose it does. It's just that I admired everything about him. The way he walked. Talked. All he needed was a cigarette and a drink and he was happy. I used to have this . . . oh, I don't know. A fantasy or something. D'you want to hear it?

Captain   Please.

Foxtrot   One night my brother asks me to go out with him. We go to a pub. Soon as we walk in, this big crowd gathers round my brother. Everyone wanted to be his mate, Captain. He was popular. You know? Anyway, someone in the pub – this girl – hits me. I don't know why. My brother turns to everyone and says, 'If you can't accept my fucking brother, then you can all rot in hell.' And he puts his arm round my shoulders and we walk out of the pub. It's a warm summer's night. We go down to the canal and throw cans into the water. My brother tells me I'm the most important thing in his life. He holds me. I smell his aftershave. Oh, God! Listen to me. Prattling on. Suppose you think I'm just a kid. But . . . I wanted this to happen so much. It never did, though. Because, one day, he met Sherbet.

Captain   Sherbet?

Foxtrot   Oh, Sherbet Gravel. His girlfriend.

Captain   Oh, yes. Of course.

Foxtrot   She was a bit of . . . Oh, I don't know the word. She was hard. She mixed with a pretty rough lot. She was a . . . a . . .

Captain   Delinquent?

Foxtrot   Cougar said you used funny words.

Captain   Delinquent's not a funny word.

Foxtrot   But I suppose she was. Gangs and stuff. You know? She used to make me nervous. Mind you, all girls made me nervous. I'm prattling on again. Just tell me to belt up. Cougar's probably told you all this anyway?

Captain   No, he hasn't. Please carry on.

Foxtrot   My brother ran away with Sherbet. We didn't see him for ages. He phoned a few times. But that's all. It's as if . . . as if we didn't exist for him any more. How can someone do that? Just forget about people?

Captain   I don't know.

Foxtrot   Anyway, one day, about two months ago . . . I was alone in the house and there was this knock on the door. It was Sherbet. She said my brother was in trouble and I had to follow her. She took me – oh, miles out. She led me down endless roads and streets and alleyways. And all the time it was getting darker and darker. She led me into a derelict building. The brickwork was all crumbling. There was no light. It smelt of piss and things. There were rats everywhere. It was like she was taking me to . . . to . . .

Captain   The Underworld.

Foxtrot   There you go with those words again.

Captain   What's wrong with them? They're perfectly descriptive.

Foxtrot   But you're right! That's just what it was like. The Underworld. Sherbet led me into a small sort of room. The room was empty, except for a pile of cardboard in the corner. And on that cardboard was . . . my brother. This must be boring you.

Captain   No.

Slight pause.

Foxtrot   My brother was so thin. His face was . . . just a skull, really. His teeth were all brown and rotting. He tried to say my name when he saw me. But he couldn't. There was blood in his mouth. Red blotches all over his skin. Like cigarette burns, but they weren't. Bruises up his arms. I thought he was going to die right there and then. We got him to hospital and . . . and . . .

Captain   Don't carry on if you don't want to.

Foxtrot   They put tubes up his nose and in his arm. He kept getting one infection after another. Half his leg rotted away. All I kept thinking was, 'Keep breathing, brov . . . Keep breathing.' Because it was as if . . . Oh, God! How can I explain? You see, going to the hospital, holding his hand, talking to him – even if he didn't hear – kept me on this planet. He was my . . . my . . .

Captain   Gravity.

Foxtrot   That's right. And, one day, my brother died and that gravity – it disappeared. I started to float up. Away from his deathbed. Up through the ceiling. It felt so peaceful. There was no feeling. Just a sense of rising higher and higher. Through the stratosphere and out into the darkness. And I would have stayed there too. Were it not for a voice calling me back. And that voice belonged to –

Captain   Cougar.

Foxtrot   Cougar! From the first time I met him, I knew he was part of me. I wanted to tell him everything about myself. My favourite films. Food. Television programmes. Computer games. Everything.

Captain   Oh, yes, yes.

Foxtrot   And I wanted to be with him all the time. Nothing was real until I told Cougar about it.

Captain   Oh, I know, yes.

Foxtrot   And all the coincidences: his date of birth. His loss of Savannah. Everything meant we were united somehow. He was my . . . my . . .

Captain   Your echo.

Foxtrot   Fuck! Yes! My echo! I lost one brother, Captain, but I found another.

Slowly, **Captain** *takes a handkerchief from his pocket. He holds handkerchief out to* **Foxtrot***.*

Foxtrot *reaches out for handkerchief.*

Just as **Foxtrot** *touches it* **Cougar** *erupts from bedroom. His hair is back in an impeccable quiff and he's wearing dark glasses again.*

Cougar   Party time!

Foxtrot   Cougar!

Foxtrot *and* **Cougar** *embrace tightly.*

Foxtrot   Oh, Cougar!

Holds embrace for while.

Then **Foxtrot** *sniffs.*

Foxtrot   Your aftershave!

Cougar   I'm wearing it for us. Us!

Foxtrot   He's wearing my brother's favourite aftershave, Captain. For us! Us!

Foxtrot *and* **Cougar** *embrace again.*

Foxtrot *hands* **Cougar** *the present.*

Foxtrot   Happy birthday, Cougar.

Cougar   A surprise? (*At* **Captain**.) Didn't I tell you he liked surprises? A present, no less.

Foxtrot   Hope you like it.

Cougar *puts present down.*

Cougar   I'll open it later. After a few drinks. Captain, start pouring! We're going to have a good party tonight.

Foxtrot   How do I look?

Cougar   Fine. Captain! Drinks!

Foxtrot   Ain't you noticed?

Cougar   Noticed what?

Foxtrot   Anything different?

Slight pause.

Captain   His hair.

Cougar   Your hair! Christ Almighty! Look at your hair!

Foxtrot   You like it?

Cougar   Course I do. Noticed it as soon as I saw you.

Foxtrot   You're kidding! I did it for you! For us! Took a hell of a long time.

Cougar   What a mate! One in a million. Where's those drinks, Captain? Us boys are dying of thirst! Right?

Foxtrot   Right! Cougar, there's . . . there's something I've got to tell you.

Cougar   Pronto, Captain! Pronto!

Foxtrot   You remember you said tonight would be our last night of grieving?

Cougar   Have you seen the cards?

Captain   Here we go.

Foxtrot   And I want it to be, Cougar. An end to . . . grief. A new start.

Cougar *hands* **Foxtrot** *some cards.* **Foxtrot** *looks at them.*

Cougar   Lots of girls wanted to come. Didn't they, Captain?

Captain   Oh, millions.

Cougar   But I told them, 'No! Tonight is for just me and my best mate.' Didn't I, Captain?

Captain   Whatever you say.

Foxtrot   Cougar! Something's happened!

Cougar   Christ Almighty, were they upset. Right, Captain?

Captain   Suicidal, I'd say.

Cougar   Don't exaggerate, Captain.

Foxtrot   I ain't had a chance to tell you!

Captain   Hurling themselves out of windows, they were.

Cougar   What's got into you?

Captain   Air full of suicidal girls. All screaming, 'I want to go to Cougar's party.'

Foxtrot   I should've told you, I know.

Cougar   I think you best go, Captain. Ain't it time for your meeting?

Captain   Oh, didn't you hear? The meeting's cancelled.

Cougar   The meeting's what?

Captain   Cancelled!

Foxtrot   Please, Cougar! Listen!

Cougar *drops cards and goes to* **Captain**.

Foxtrot *picks up cards.*

Cougar   The meeting's never fucking cancelled. Now just fuck off. I need my buzz!

Captain   Your buzz is not going to happen!

Foxtrot   Cougar!

Cougar   Not going to . . . I'll fucking kill you, Captain. I swear I will.

Captain   I am not leaving you alone so you can lead that lamb to the slaughter.

Foxtrot   Please, Cougar! Captain! I have to explain something important!

Cougar *opens door to corridor He doesn't see* **Sherbet Gravel** *standing in doorway.*

Cougar   Fuck off, Captain!

Sherbet *is seventeen years old. Her hair and her clothes are stylishly streetwise. She is clutching a handbag.*

Foxtrot *sees* **Sherbet**.

Foxtrot   Oh, God!

Captain *sees* **Sherbet**.

Cougar (*at* **Captain**)   I'll skin you alive!

Captain (*indicating* **Sherbet**)   Cougar!

Cougar *turns to see* **Sherbet**.

Sherbet   Hello, all!

Foxtrot   You were supposed to wait downstairs.

Sherbet   I did wait, Babe. Then I got fucked off with waiting.

Foxtrot   What's the point of making a plan if you don't – ?

Sherbet   Happy birthday, Cougar!

Foxtrot   This . . . this is what I've been trying to tell you. Cougar, Captain, this is Sherbet.

Lights flicker off and on.

Sound of crackling electricity.

Sherbet   Tell them, Babe.

Foxtrot   Sherbet is *my* girlfriend now.

Lights flicker off and on.

Sound of crackling electricity.

Captain   Good Lord!

Sherbet   Tell them, Babe.

Foxtrot   And she's going to have my baby.

Lights flicker off and on.

Sound of crackling electricity.

Captain   Good Lord!

Foxtrot   And –

Sherbet   We're going to be married!

Sherbet *holds* **Foxtrot's** *hand.*

Lights flicker off and on.

Sound of crackling electricity.

Slight pause.

Sherbet   Ain't come at a bad time, have I?

Slight pause.

Captain   Bad time? No, Sherbet. Not at all. Whoever heard the like? You can't imagine how welcome you are. Come in! Stay!

Captain *closes door behind* **Sherbet**.

Lights flicker very violently now.

Electricity also crackles very violently.

Captain   Damn these lights! But – Good Lord! What does it matter? We're going to have a party! Who needs light?

Blackout.

Act Two

Darkness.

Captain *enters from bedroom holding birthday cake and large knife.*

All the candles are lit, illuminating the room.

Cougar, **Foxtrot** *and* **Sherbet** *are sitting round the table.*

Captain (*brightly singing*)
Happy birthday to you . . .

All (*except* **Cougar**, *singing*)
Happy birthday to you,
Happy birthday, dear Cougar,
Happy birthday to you.

Sherbet *claps enthusiastically.*

Foxtrot *joins in.*

Captain *puts cake on table.*

Sherbet   Fucking hell, what a beautiful cake. It looks so traditional. I love traditional things. Don't I, Babe?

Foxtrot   You do, Babe.

Cougar *offers* **Captain** *some vodka.* **Captain** *refuses.*

Sherbet   I never used to. But now I can't get enough of them.

Cougar *offers* **Sherbet** *some vodka.* **Sherbet** *refuses.*

Sherbet   No thanks, Cougar. I don't touch poisons now. Do I, Babe?

Foxtrot   You don't, Babe.

Sherbet   Ah, yes. Traditional things. Cake on birthdays. Eggs at Easter.

Cougar *offers* **Foxtrot** *some vodka.*

Sherbet   Babe don't either. Do you, Babe?

Foxtrot   Er . . . no, Babe.

Cougar *glares at* **Foxtrot***, then starts drinking from bottle.*

Sherbet   And Christmas! Ooooh, I love everything to do
with Christmas. It's time for the family. Getting together.
Turkey. Christmas pudding. Watching television all afternoon.
Usually a big film. Cartoons. Singing Christmas carols. Turkey
sandwiches. And then New Year. Midnight chimes. Arm in
arm. 'May old acquaintance be forgot' and all that. A few tears.
Making resolutions. Christmas and New Year are times for the
family. I never used to believe that. But I've changed. The past
year has taught me a lot. About the value of traditional things.

Cougar *burps.* **Foxtrot** *laughs.*

Sherbet   Manners, Mr Glass. Manners. Don't laugh, Babe.

Foxtrot   Sorry, Babe.

Sherbet   Babe has still got a few things to learn. But don't
worry. I'm teaching him. You know the first thing I taught
him? How to propose.

Foxtrot   Don't, Babe.

Sherbet   Don't be bashful, Babe. We're amongst friends.
You know what I made him do? Go down on one knee –

Foxtrot *(softly, overlapping)*   Oh, God.

Sherbet *(overlapping)*   – and say, 'Please, Miss Gravel, may
I have your hand in marriage?' And I said, 'You may.' He's
blushing. Look at him. Bless him. But it's the gospel truth. You
know what kind of wedding we're going to have?

Captain   A traditional one?

Sherbet   Bingo! Not a traditional white wedding, mind you.
Because it's not traditional for a pregnant woman to walk down
the aisle. But a traditional registry office wedding. People will
still wear posh clothes and throw confetti, though. Then we'll
have a lovely reception. Salmon and cucumber sandwiches.

Little sausages on sticks. And a big cake, three tiers high. Babe and I, we'll hold the knife and cut the cake together. That's supposed to be good luck, I hear.

Captain   Oh, it is.

Sherbet   And then . . . then, you know what we'll have? Tell them, Babe.

Foxtrot   A honeymoon!

Sherbet   Somewhere hot! And then we'll settle down in a . . . Babe?

Foxtrot   A traditional house.

Sherbet   Little garden out front.

Foxtrot   Little garden out back.

Sherbet   And we'll have a nursery.

Foxtrot   Blue if it's a boy.

Sherbet   Pink if it's a girl.

Foxtrot   And Babe'll do the cooking.

Sherbet   Roast beef on Sunday.

Foxtrot   Roast potatoes.

Sherbet   Yorkshire pudding.

Foxtrot   Mustard!

Sherbet   And Babe will have a steady job.

Foxtrot   Nine to five.

Sherbet   While I do the housework.

Foxtrot   Bring up baby.

Sherbet   Teach it the ABC.

Foxtrot   Nursery rhymes.

Sherbet   How to count.

Foxtrot   Use the toilet.

Sherbet   And the value of traditional things!

Foxtrot (*with* **Sherbet**)   . . . value of traditional things!

Captain   Good Lord! I'm breathless just listening to you both!

Sherbet   But don't it sound idyllic, Captain?

Captain   Absolute heaven.

Slight pause.

Sherbet   Fucking hell! The engagement ring! I ain't shown you the ring! Now, you all know what to do. I hold out me hand and you make suitable 'ooh' and 'ahh' noises. Ready? Here goes!

Shows ring to **Captain**.

Captain   It's divine, Sherbet. Absolutely divine.

Sherbet   Very good, Captain. You pass the test with flying fucking colours.

Shows ring to **Cougar**.

Cougar *doesn't react.*

Sherbet   Suitable 'oohs' and 'ahhs', if you please.

Cougar *still doesn't react.*

Sherbet   Cougar's a little skimpy in the 'ooh' and 'ahh' department.

Foxtrot   Don't you like it, Cougar?

Captain   He's been in a barbaric mood all evening.

Sherbet   Don't make such a fuss, you two. I know what it is. It's those old birthday blues. Nineteen must be one of those birthdays. Just one more year left of being a teenager. Soon you'll be an old man. With responsibilities and the suchlike. I knew it might take something special to get you in the party mood. So I came prepared.

Picks up handbag.

The handbag!

Opens handbag.

In this bag I've got everything we need.

Reaches into handbag.

Slight pause.

Whips hats out of handbag.

Party hats!

Captain   Good Lord!

Foxtrot   What a surprise!

Sherbet   Now there's one for everyone. Here you are, Babe.

Gives hat to **Foxtrot**.

Foxtrot   It'll mess up my hair, Babe.

Sherbet   Don't be a fusspot. It's a party. Let yourself go, Babe.

Foxtrot   But I did my hair just for Cougar.

Sherbet   *I* did your hair, Babe. Came straight round to the salon after school he did. Do my hair! Do my hair! Anyone would think his life depended on it. Only just finished it in time, I did. Oh, look at him. Bless! I could eat you up! Yum, yum! Put it on!

Foxtrot *puts hat on.*

Sherbet   Captain, this one's for you.

Captain   Thank you.

Sherbet *gives hat to* **Captain**.

Captain *puts it on.*

Sherbet *puts a hat on. Then –*

Sherbet   And this one's for the Birthday Boy.

Holds hat out to **Cougar**.

Sherbet   Go on! Put it on!

Cougar *does not move*.

Slight pause.

Sherbet   You know what I think? I think Cougar's a little tiddly. Am I right? That's what you get for drinking straight out the bottle! I know. I'll put the hat on for you.

Foxtrot   He doesn't like anyone touching his hair, Babe.

Sherbet   Well, if he doesn't like it, he'll stop me, won't he?

Starts putting hat on **Cougar**.

Sherbet   He'll slap me out of the way and say, 'Don't touch my hair.' Won't you, Birthday Boy? You'll slap me so fucking hard my skull will split in two and all my brains will spill out over the fucking floor.

Finishes putting hat on **Cougar**.

Sherbet   There you are! Oh, look at you! Ha! You know what you look like? A rabbit caught in car headlights. Don't he, Babe?

Foxtrot   He does a bit, I guess.

Laughs.

Sherbet   Captain? Don't you think he looks like a rabbit caught in car headlights?

Captain   Yes, yes indeed.

Laughs.

Sherbet   A rabbit in car headlights. Frozen stiff by the dazzle. Waiting for the car to run it over. Bless him . . . Oh, well, at least that's eased the atmosphere a little bit, ain't it? I'm feeling quite relaxed now. You, Babe?

Foxtrot   I am, Babe.

Sherbet   You best be careful, Captain. If I make myself too much at home, you'll never get rid of me.

Captain   You'd be most welcome, Sherbet.

Sherbet   Listen to that, Babe!

Foxtrot   What, Babe?

Sherbet   He's flirting with me. Ain't ya, Captain?

Captain   Well, I wouldn't say I –

Sherbet   You should stand up for me, Babe. Protect my honour. The Captain might want to have his wicked way with me. Right, Captain?

Captain   Why not? You're such a ravishing creature.

Sherbet   Ravishing! You hear that, Babe? You should get a gun and blow his fucking brains out.

Foxtrot   What?

Sherbet   You'd protect me if someone was out to ravish me, wouldn't you? . . . Wouldn't you, Babe?

Foxtrot   Course I would, Babe. Goes without saying.

Sherbet   Because I'd do the same for you. If anyone was out to ravish you, I'd do anything to protect you. I'd rip out their fucking heart with my bare hands before they had a chance to pluck one single hair from your head.

Foxtrot   Oh, God, Babe.

Sherbet   Babe.

Foxtrot *and* **Sherbet** *embrace and kiss.*

Cougar *grabs knife on table and lifts it in air.*

Captain   Cougar! No!

Foxtrot *and* **Sherbet** *jump apart.*

Sherbet   Fucking hell!

Foxtrot   What's going on?

Captain   No, Cougar, no.

Slight pause.

Sherbet   The Captain's right, Cougar. You can't cut the cake yet. You've got to blow the candles out first. Right, Captain?

Captain   Absolutely.

Sherbet   You make a wish, then blow out all the candles. And if you manage to get all the candles out, your wish comes true.

Foxtrot   But you have to do it in one breath.

Sherbet   That's right.

Foxtrot   And something else.

Sherbet   Something else?

Foxtrot   Something you have to do to make your wish come true.

Sherbet   Is it traditional, Babe?

Foxtrot   Very traditional, Babe.

Sherbet   What can it be? Make a wish. Blow out the candles.

Captain   I know! I know!

Sherbet   So there really *is* something else?

Foxtrot   I said there was. I'm not stupid.

Sherbet   Didn't say you was, Babe. Fucking hell, what can it be?

Slight pause.

Foxtrot   Give up?

Sherbet   All right. I give up.

Foxtrot   Captain?

Captain   Never tell anyone your wish.

Foxtrot   That's it! That's it!

Sherbet   Fucking hell. Of course. Of all the things to forget.

Foxtrot   Well done, Captain.

Sherbet   Now, Cougar. You know all the rules. Blow candles out. Use only one breath to do it. And never tell anyone your wish. On the count of three, fill those lungs and give us a tornado! Ready? One . . . two . . . three!

Cougar *doesn't move. He toys with knife.*

Pause.

Sherbet   The party hat don't seem to have helped much, does it? Come on, everyone. Let's give him some encouragement. We'll say it together . . .

All (*except* **Cougar**)   One . . . two . . . three!

Cougar *doesn't move.*

Foxtrot   Why ain't you making a wish, Cougar?

Pause.

Sherbet   I know why. Because he's got everything! Nothing left to wish for. Lucky ol' Cougar. Right, Babe?

Foxtrot   Lucky ol' Cougar.

Slight pause.

Sherbet   Wish I was lucky enough not to want a wish. What about you, Captain? If you could have one wish, what would it be?

Captain   Good Lord! I don't know.

Sherbet   But you must have one.

Captain   Well . . . yes, I have.

Foxtrot   Tell us, Captain.

Captain   I don't know if I can.

Sherbet   Oh, bless him. You're amongst friends, Captain.

Foxtrot   Please, Captain. Please.

Slight pause.

Captain   Hair.

Slight pause.

I was eighteen when my hair started to fall out.

Foxtrot   Eighteen! You're fucking kidding!

Sherbet   Shush, Babe. Go on, Captain.

Captain   At first, I thought it was just a phase. I thought it would grow back. I went to see a doctor. He said nothing could be done. My hair would never grow back. I became suicidal. I was going . . . I couldn't even say the word! I still find it difficult. Once I knew it was happening, I became obsessed with hair. Suddenly, everywhere I went people were talking about hair. How they were going to grow it, cut it, bleach it, perm it, dye it, streak it. When I walked down the street, I didn't look at people's faces or what they were wearing. I just looked at their hair. And when I thought of the future, I didn't think, 'By then I'll be doing this,' or, 'By then I'll be doing that.' I just thought, 'By then I'll be . . . bald.' You don't know what it's like the first time someone says, 'You're going bald!' And it's said like an accusation. As if it's something you've done. Your fault in some way. Something deficient in your diet. And then the accusatory tone goes and it's replaced with something worse. Amusement! And they're laughing. They find it funny. Hysterical. All your suicidal thoughts, your nights of tears, your hours counting dead hairs. It doesn't mean anything to them. All they're thinking is, 'Glad it's not me.' And, 'Doesn't he look ugly?'

Sherbet   But . . . you don't look ugly at all.

Captain   Oh, take no notice of me.

Sherbet   Captain ain't ugly, is he, Babe?

Foxtrot   No.

Sherbet   You're beautiful, Captain. A beauty that has fuck-all to do with hair or suntan or what you wear. A beauty that will never age. Don't you think so, Cougar?

Slight pause.

Cougar *violently blows candles out.*

His sudden movement makes everyone jump and yelp out loud.

Captain   Cougar!

Sherbet   Fucking hell!

Foxtrot   Oh, God, Cougar! You made me bloody jump!

Sherbet   Me, too, I can tell you.

Captain   He did it on purpose.

Slight pause.

Sherbet   Well, at least he made a wish, bless him. The hat must be working after all.

Pause.

We haven't got to sit here in the dark, have we, Captain?

Captain   Don't panic. There's a candelabrum at the ready.

Foxtrot   Captain Tock to the rescue!

Captain *goes to candelabrum and starts lighting candles.*

Sherbet   I love candelabrums. They're so –

Foxtrot   Traditional.

Sherbet   No, Babe. Romantic. Right, Captain?

Captain *lights candelabrum.*

Captain   Well, it all depends where you are, I suppose.

Pause.

One day I lit this candelabrum and went downstairs to the abandoned factory.

Holds candelabrum aloft.

And I opened a door I had never opened before.

Sherbet   Ooo, Captain. I'm gripped already. Did you go inside?

Captain   I did. It was very dark. I lifted the candelabrum. And I looked.

Sherbet   What can you see?

Captain   The universe! I'm floating in space. Around me are millions of stars, all tinged with orange, zodiac after zodiac, all glowing like tiny sparks. And then . . . then I see other things. Things between the stars. Silver things glinting. Tiny hooks. Tiny daggers. Suddenly the universe is not a safe place to be. And the stars begin to move. And . . . and I hear a noise. The noise is all round me. A noise I've never heard before. Strange bird calls . . .

Sherbet *begins to make gentle haunting bird calls.* **Foxtrot** *follows her lead.*

Captain   And then I see. The stars are not stars. They're eyes. Birds' eyes. And the hooks are not hooks. They're claws. And the daggers are beaks. The noise . . . the noise gets louder . . .

The bird calls from **Foxtrot** *and* **Sherbet** *get louder.*

Captain   Then I begin to see other things. Cages. Knives. Scissors. Electric wire. It's like a torture chamber. That's all the universe is. One big torture chamber.

The lights come on.

Foxtrot   Light!

Sherbet   Bingo! You're dripping wax on the floor, Captain.

Captain   Good Lord! Thank you.

Captain *blows candles out and puts candelabrum down.*

Sherbet   Now I can have a proper look at the place.

Looks round.

You like your birds, don't you, Captain?

Captain   They're a bit of an obsession, yes.

Sherbet   More than a bit, I'd say . . . Ooo, Babe, look at that one's feathers. Ain't they beautiful?

Foxtrot   Beautiful, Babe.

Captain   They use them in mating rituals. To attract a partner.

Sherbet   So feathers are all about fucking, are they, Captain?

Captain   They're all about perpetuating the species. Survival.

Sherbet   You know what gets me about birds? Their faces. They never show any feeling, do they? I bet you could put a bird through a mangle feet first and the look on its face wouldn't change one jot.

Continues to look round.

Fucking hell, look at the walls. Just like living in − what was it Cougar said, Babe? A huge cracked egg.

Captain   That's my expression. I said that.

Sherbet   You said Cougar said it, Babe.

Foxtrot   I did, but −

Captain   They're my words. I've been saying them for years.

Sherbet   Naughty fibber, Mr Glass.

Foxtrot   Perhaps I misheard.

Sherbet   Think so, Babe?

Foxtrot   Probably, yeah.

Sherbet   In that case, I'm sorry, Cougar. I shouldn't have called you a liar. I'm sure you wouldn't have deliberately misled my Babe. Misleading people is a shocking thing to do.

Slight pause.

Captain   Why don't you two tell me your wishes? After all, I've told you mine. What would yours be, Foxtrot?

Foxtrot   Oh, God. I don't know. What about you, Babe?

Sherbet   Well, in a way I've got everything I could ever wish for in this very room. My fiancé. A baby on the way. Good friends. What more can I wish for? But . . . well, but I do, I'm ashamed to say.

Foxtrot   What, Babe?

Sherbet   Tell us yours first, Babe.

Foxtrot   No. You, Babe.

Sherbet   You, Babe.

Foxtrot   You, Babe.

Sherbet   You, Babe.

Foxtrot   You, Babe.

Sherbet   You, Babe.

Foxtrot   But I don't know. I've never thought about it.

Sherbet   Bless him. Think about it.

Pause.

Foxtrot   Whiskers! That's it. Whiskers! I like the idea of coming home drunk at night, falling asleep with my clothes on, and waking up in the morning with stubble. My brother has very thick whiskers. *Had* very thick whiskers. And I like the idea of shaving and putting on lots of aftershave. My brother's favourite. Yeah, that's it. Whiskers! That's my wish.

Sherbet   But that ain't a proper wish, Babe.

Foxtrot   It is. It's what I want.

Captain   What Sherbet is saying is that . . . well, whiskers are bound to happen. It's like wishing for . . . oh, I don't know . . .

Sherbet   Wrinkles.

Captain   Exactly.

Foxtrot   How come?

Sherbet   Well, wrinkles are inevitable, Babe. When you wish for something, it should be something that might not be possible.

Foxtrot   Some men don't get whiskers.

Sherbet   Very few, Babe.

Foxtrot   It's possible.

Sherbet   But not probable.

Foxtrot   What's the difference?

Captain   Well, possible means it −

Foxtrot   Oh, God! I don't want a bloody argument.

Sherbet   We're not arguing, Babe.

Foxtrot   You are! It's only a fucking game. Didn't know there was a long list of rules and regulations about making a bloody wish. Why turn it all into a . . . a . . . ? − I wish for whiskers! That's it! Don't want no fucking lecture!

Pause.

Sherbet   Who wants to know my wish?

Captain   Me, please.

Sherbet   Babe?

Foxtrot   What?

Sherbet   Do you want to know my wish?

Slight pause.

Babe?

Slight pause.

Babe?

Foxtrot   Yeah, all right.

Sherbet   Yeah, all right what?

Foxtrot   Yeah, all right . . . Babe.

Sherbet   I wish to grow old gracefully. Now I know that sounds ridiculous, but I've seen enough people not doing it gracefully to know exactly what I'm talking about. The beauty salon where I work is full of them. Men and women. All with the same look in their eyes. Make me young. But you know something? There's nothing we can do. Nature has rules and regulations and most of them are either cruel or fucking cruel. You know, I can usually tell a person's age as easy as that! One look is all it takes.

Looks at **Cougar**.

Cougar *backs away.*

Sherbet   There's this one woman who comes in – I feel sorry for her in a way – and she's got this photograph of what she looked like when she was nineteen. She must be – oh, sixty if she's a bloody day now. Anyway, she comes in and she shows me this photo and – fucking hell! – was she beautiful! 'This was me,' she says. It's as if that photograph captured her at the happiest moment of her life. Perhaps it's like that. Perhaps we reach our peak when we're nineteen and, for one glorious summer, we're in control of our lives, and we look wonderful and everything is perfect. And then it's never the same again. And we spend the rest of our lives merely surviving one empty summer after another.

Captain   Oh, I . . . I don't think it's like that at all. You might not live that same summer again, but others are glorious for different reasons.

Sherbet   I'm sure you're right, Captain. Anyway, I ain't afraid of getting old. It's only natural.

Cougar *goes over to sofa.*

Captain (*at* **Cougar**)   If you're not in the party mood, why don't you just leave?

Cougar *glares at* **Captain**.

Sherbet   Ooo, what a look.

Captain   He won't go.

Foxtrot   Why should he? It's *his* party.

Sherbet   Grumpy, Mr Glass.

Captain   If you can't have your own way, you'll just spoil it for everyone else, won't you!

Foxtrot   He's not spoiling it for me.

Captain   Well, he is for me.

Foxtot   Well, he ain't for me!

Sherbet   Now, now, now! Let's not make too much of it. We're supposed to be having fun and games. But, don't worry, handbag to the rescue!

Holds handbag up.

I told you, I've got everything in here to put us in a party mood.

Puts hand in bag.

Can you guess what I've got this time?

Slight pause.

No?

Pulls out plastic glasses with false noses attached.

Masks! Well, almost masks. Plastic glasses with noses. But they were so funny, I just had to get them. Captain, this one's for you.

Captain   Thank you.

Puts mask on.

Sherbet   Babe, this is for you.

Foxtrot   Thanks, Babe.

Puts mask on.

Sherbet   I said we'd have a good party, didn't I, Babe? One way or another. Ooo, Babe! Look at Captain!

Laughs.

Foxtrot   Oh, God! Captain!

Laughs.

Sherbet   And look at you, Babe! You look just as funny!

Foxtrot   You're kidding! Do I?

Captain   Good Lord, yes!

Sherbet   Don't make me laugh too much. The Future One will start fluttering.

Puts mask on.

How do I look?

Foxtrot *and* **Captain** *laugh.*

Foxtrot   Suits you, Babe.

Sherbet   Don't push your luck.

Captain   He's right, Sherbet. It does.

Sherbet   You're wicked, you two!

Holds out final mask.

And this one is for Birthday Boy.

Takes mask to **Cougar**.

Sherbet   Come on, Cougar!

Captain   Yes, put it on.

Sherbet   Get in the party mood, for fuck's sake.

Cougar *doesn't react.*

Slight pause.

Sherbet   Shall I put it on for you?

Foxtrot   I don't really think it's his thing, Babe.

Sherbet   You know what I think it is. I think it's all the drink. Made him a little numb, bless him . . . I'll put the mask on for him.

Takes off **Cougar**'s *sunglasses.*

Cougar *stares at* **Sherbet**.

Slight pause.

Slowly, **Sherbet** *starts to put mask on* **Cougar**.

Cougar *plays with knife.*

Sherbet   We'll all wear masks. Our faces will be hidden. Who knows what we're thinking? Or what we might do? My, anything could happen. Anything at all.

The mask is on.

Sherbet   There! What d'you think?

Laughs.

Captain   A definite improvement.

Sherbet   I think so too. You should keep it on. Then you'll have even more girls after you.

Foxtrot (*laughing, at* **Cougar**)   It does look funny.

Sherbet   I bet all these cards are from your female admirers, Cougar.

Picks up card.

I was right! Tracy!

Picks up another card.

And this one? Lesley. Oh, yeah.

Looks at more cards.

Yeah! Yeah! Just as I thought. Your little harem. I would have thought they'd be here tonight. Would have been nice for me, if nothing else. To have some girls to natter with. Could have asked them why they all used the same pen to start with. Perhaps they all wrote them together. As a group. I know that's what me and my friends used to do on Valentine's Day. All get together for a mammoth card-writing session. Fucking hell, that was fun. Mind you, I was young then.

Captain   Good Lord! You're young now. You can't be more than . . . what? Eighteen?

Sherbet   Seventeen! But I'm getting on, Captain. Only a few years left of being a teenager. Fuck, it must be hell not to be a teenager. Cougar knows what I mean. Only one year left for him. And look, he's hardly a bundle of laughs, is he?

Foxtrot   That ain't fair, Babe.

Sherbet   What? Oh, I'm sorry, Babe. Of course it's not. Sorry, Cougar. You've been through so much. Losing your poor wife like that. I know what it's like. But you've got to make an effort. It's your birthday. You know . . . Cake! Funny hats! Pres – Fucking hell! The present! You ain't even opened your present yet.

Foxtrot   Forgot all about it.

Captain   So did I.

Sherbet *puts present in* **Cougar***'s lap.*

Sherbet   There you are!

Foxtrot   Babe chose it.

Sherbet   It was you as well, Babe.

Foxtrot   You really, Babe.

Sherbet   *Both* of us chose it. Now, go on. Open it.

Foxtrot   Yeah. Open it.

Pause.

Slowly, **Cougar** *cuts away wrapping paper with knife.*

Sherbet   Knew that knife would come in handy.

Foxtrot   Hope you like it, Cougar.

Sits next to **Cougar** *on sofa.*

Sherbet   Of course he'll like it. Come closer, Captain. You don't want to miss the look on his face when he sees it.

Captain *comes closer.*

Sherbet   Look at him. He can hardly contain his excitement, bless him.

Cougar *grudgingly opens present to reveal a clock.*

Sherbet   A clock!

Captain   Good Lord!

Foxtrot   D'you like it?

Cougar *is trembling, clutching the knife.*

Captain   Give it to me.

Takes clock from **Cougar**.

Captain   I've got just the place for this.

Foxtrot   I knew he wouldn't like it.

Captain   I'm sure he does.

Sherbet   Not so much as a thank you.

Captain   Gratitude isn't one of his strongest points – There!

Puts clock on mantelpiece.

Sherbet   Shame on you, Mr Glass! Shame!

Foxtrot (*at* **Cougar**)   I wanted to get you this ring I saw. A silver crocodile.

Sherbet   You ain't buying him a fucking ring.

Foxtrot   It's better than a fucking clock.

Captain   I know a story about a clock.

Cougar *stares at* **Captain**.

Slight pause.

Sherbet   Do you? Ooo, I love stories. So do you, don't you, Babe?

Foxtrot   Er . . . yeah.

Sherbet   Tell us the story, Captain.

Cougar *glares at* **Captain**.

Captain   Good Lord, I . . . I don't know. Perhaps I shouldn't have mentioned it.

Sherbet   No, no, no. Tell us! Here. I'll sit down.

Sherbet *sits on floor in front of* **Foxtrot** *and* **Cougar**.

Sherbet   We're your captive audience. Where's the story come from?

Captain   I . . . I made it up.

Foxtrot   Oh, God. You're kidding!

Sherbet   That does it! You've got to tell us now, Captain. Ain't he, Babe?

Foxtrot   He has, Babe. No arguments, Captain. Come on!

Pause.

Captain *faces them.*

Captain   I . . . I made this up many years ago. For someone I met. Someone . . . someone I cared for a great deal. Someone who did not care for me.

Sherbet   That's the worst thing in the world.

Captain   Yes, it is. And so . . . this story came into my head. I don't know where it came from. One day it was I there, as if it had always been there.

Sherbet   Oh, tell us, Captain.

Foxtrot   Yeah. *Please*, Captain.

Pause.

Captain   Once, a long time ago, there lived the most beautiful Prince in the world –

Cougar *yawns loudly.*

Slight pause.

Captain   Everywhere he went people followed him, content merely to be near him. Every morning the Prince would look at the sunrise and say, 'I am more adored than you, because there are some who burn easily in your light.'

Cougar *feigns sleep and starts to snore.*

Captain   And every night the Prince would look at the stars and say, 'I am more adored than any of you, because there are some who despise the dark that you need to shine.'

Cougar*'s snoring gets louder.*

Sherbet   Less noise in the peanut gallery, if you please.

Foxtrot *nudges* **Cougar**.

Cougar *continues snoring.*

Captain   And so it went on. The Prince roamed the land, adored by all who saw him. 'How stupid people are,' said the Prince. 'I am their world, yet they mean nothing to me.'

Cougar*'s snoring gets louder.*

Sherbet   Fucking hell.

Foxtrot   Cougar!

Foxtrot *nudges* **Cougar**, *laughing.*

Sherbet   It's not funny, Babe.

Foxtrot   Didn't say it was.

Sherbet   Why you laughing, then?

Captain   Let him snore if he wants to! Ignore him.

Slight pause.

And then, one day, the Prince met a Wizard. The Prince told the Wizard how he was adored by everyone and how funny he found it. Because the Prince cared for no one. The Wizard said, 'You might be the most beautiful thing in the world, but you are also the most cruel. Your face shows no expression. It is hard and emotionless. Like the face of a vulture. To punish you, I will put a spell on you.'

Cougar *continues snoring.*

Captain *(suddenly shouting)*   Quiet, Cougar! Quiet!

Cougar *feigns 'waking up'.*

Sherbet   You're missing a really good story, Cougar. You shouldn't have drunk so much. Oh, carry on, Captain. What was the spell? Something fucking nasty, I hope.

Cougar *encourages* **Foxtrot** *to take several large swigs from the vodka bottle as –*

Captain   The Wizard changed the Prince's face into the face of a vulture. His hair fell out and was replaced with feathers. His nose grew longer and harder and turned into a beak. The Prince screamed and screamed and begged the Wizard to give him back his beautiful face. 'No,' said the Wizard. 'The only thing that will save you is when you find the Fastest Clock in the Universe.'

Cougar *reaches down and gets the pornographic magazine from under the sofa.*

Captain   And so the Prince wandered the land. He looked everywhere for the Fastest Clock. But what was it? What did it look like? Was it big or small?

Cougar *begins flicking through the magazine.*

Foxtrot *looks at magazine.*

Captain   He asked everyone he met. But when they saw his feathered-face they ran away, screaming, 'Go back to hell, you vulture!'

Foxtrot *points at photo.*

Cougar *turns page.*

Captain   Years passed –

Sherbet   Oh, what a lovely phrase. Years passed. Sorry, Captain.

Foxtrot *turns page in magazine.*

He lets out a gasp as he sees a photo and smiles at Cougar.

Captain   One day, while he was looking for food in a forest, the Prince met a girl. The Prince went up to the girl and said, 'I am weak and hungry. Will you help?' And the girl replied, 'Of course.'

Sherbet   I bet she was blind.

Captain   That's right. The girl was blind.

Sherbet   Did the Prince tell the Blind Girl about his search the Fastest Clock?

Captain   Yes, he did.

Sherbet   And she knew where to find it?

Captain   No. But she said she would help him search. The sound of his crying had touched her heart.

Foxtrot *gasps at another photo.*

Sherbet   Where did they search, Captain?

Captain   Everywhere. One day, while they were walking through a forest, the Prince's foot got caught in a steel trap. The trap clasped round the Prince's ankle like steel jaws.

Sherbet   Fucking hell!

Captain   Using all her strength, the Blind Girl tried to open the trap. But she couldn't.

Foxtrot *takes another swig from bottle.*

Cougar *starts to stroke* **Foxtrot***'s hair.*

Sherbet   Get help! Get help!

Captain   Oh, she did. She ran through the forest until she found a man chopping down a tree. She asked him to follow her. He did so. But when the man saw the vulture-face of the Prince, he screamed.

Foxtrot *snuggles up very close to* **Cougar**.

He is getting more and more turned on.

Cougar *removes their masks and hats, then puts his hand on* **Foxtrot**'s *knee and squeezes.*

Sherbet   Stupid fucking man!

Captain   'It's a terrible creature,' he said. 'And it deserves to die!' And the man lifted his axe into the air.

Sherbet   No!

Cougar *begins to feel along* **Foxtrot**'s *leg.*

Foxtrot *opens his legs.*

Captain   The Blind Girl shielded the Prince from the axe, shouting at the man, 'I won't let you hurt one feather on his head!'

Cougar's *hand is almost on* **Foxtrot**'s *crotch.*

Sherbet   Yes! One feather on his fucking head!

Captain   The man with the axe said, 'If you want to protect a monster like this, then you must be a monster too.' And again the man lifted his axe into the air to strike the Blind Girl.

Sherbet   No!

Cougar *begins rubbing* **Foxtrot**'s *crotch.*

Captain   And now . . . now the Prince struggled up – it caused him great pain – and he shielded the Blind Girl from the axe, shouting at the man, 'I won't let you hurt one hair on her head.'

Sherbet   Oh, it's so romantic.

Cougar loosens Foxtrot's trousers.

Captain   And then . . . the Prince started to change. The feathers and beak disappeared. And he . . . he became the most beautiful thing in the universe again. And . . . and he and the Blind Girl lived together for the rest of their lives.

Sherbet   So the vulture face had gone?

Captain   Yes.

Sherbet   Oh, beautiful.

Cougar's *hand slips into* **Foxtrot**'s *trousers.*

Captain   Because at that moment, when they thought they were going to lose each other . . . they . . . found . . .

Cougar *is masturbating* **Foxtrot**.

Captain   . . . the Fastest Clock in the Universe

Foxtrot *moans gently.*

Captain *jumps to his feet.*

Captain   Stop it! Stop it!

Foxtrot *jumps to his feet.*

Sherbet *looks round.*

Foxtrot   What's the problem? What?

Hurriedly does up trousers.

Sherbet   Babe? What you – ?

Sees magazine.

Fucking hell! You looking at this, Babe?

Picks up magazine.

Foxtrot   A little bit, yeah.

Cougar *and* **Foxtrot** *start giggling.*

Sherbet (*at* **Cougar**)   Where was this hidden?

Captain (*at* **Cougar**)   You won't give up, will you?!

Foxtrot   It's only a bit of a laugh. Don't make such a fuss.

Sherbet   It's disgusting.

Foxtrot   Says who?

Sherbet   Says me!

Foxtrot   Ooo, the mighty Sherbet has spoken!

Sherbet   What's that supposed to mean?

Foxtrot   Perhaps I'm fed up with all your fucking opinions. You thought of that? Eh? Perhaps I'm not ready for all your fucking boring traditional things and if you don't like it you can just fuck off.

Long pause.

Cougar *puts sunglasses back on. He grins at* **Sherbet**.

Slight pause.

Sherbet *clutches her stomach.*

Sherbet   Fucking hell.

Captain   What's wrong, Sherbet?

Sherbet   It's nothing, Captain.

Captain   Sit down.

Captain *helps* **Sherbet** *sit.*

Captain   Is it the baby?

Sherbet   Don't make a fuss now. The Future One is only moving about. Heard its dad shouting, I reckon.

Captain   I think the whole street heard its dad shouting.

Sherbet   It's all right, Future One. Your daddy's not angry with you – Ooo, it's kicking. Want to feel, Captain?

Captain   Can I?

Sherbet *lays* **Captain**'s *hand on her stomach.*

Slight pause.

Sherbet   There!

Captain   Remarkable.

Foxtrot   Let me.

Approaches **Sherbet**.

Sherbet   Sure you want to? Daddies feeling their Future One is a very traditional thing.

Foxtrot   I want to, Babe. Please.

Puts his hand on **Sherbet***'s stomach.*

Foxtrot *gasps and laughs as he feels a kick.*

Foxtrot   Oh, yesss! Yesss!

Sherbet *strokes his hair and grins at* **Cougar**.

Sherbet   Babe cares so much for the Future One.

Captain   Oh, I can see that.

Slight pause.

Sherbet   I've got myself a job and a fiancé – all in two months. How's that for survival, eh, Captain?

Captain   Very impressive.

Sherbet   I deserve a bit of bloody happiness after all I've been through. And the Future One is still Babe's flesh and blood. You understand?

Captain   Yes, yes, I understand.

Foxtrot   We're going to name the Future One after my brother.

Captain   You know it's a boy then?

Foxtrot   Oh, yeah. We've seen it. Ain't we, Babe?

Sherbet   Yes, Babe. On a screen.

Captain   A screen?

Foxtrot   A scanner.

Sherbet   In the hospital.

Foxtrot   . . . Millions of spots of light. Like . . . like . . .

Captain   Constellations?

Foxtrot   Yeah! Constellations.

Captain   Constellations of arms?

Foxtrot   And legs.

Sherbet   And toes.

Captain   And the head was like . . . Jupiter?

Sherbet   Oh, yes!

Captain   And you could see its eyes?

Foxtrot   Yeah! Its eyes . . . eyes like . . . like two moons!

Captain   And the veins across its skull?

Foxtrot   The tails of comets!

Captain   Its ears?

Sherbet   Craters.

Captain   Craters of?

Foxtrot   Craters of?

Sherbet   Meteors!

Captain   Very good!

Sherbet   Ancient meteors!

Captain   Better still! Bravo, Sherbet.

Captain and **Foxtrot** *applaud.*

Sherbet   I'm really having a good time! Are you, Babe?

Foxtrot   I am, Babe.

Sherbet and **Foxtrot** *hold hands.*

Captain   I wasn't going to eat any cake. But now . . . now
I think I will. The icing looks so tempting. Perhaps I should
cut it.

Sherbet   Let Cougar cut it, Captain.

Foxtrot   It's bad luck if anyone else does it.

Captain   I know, but I –

Sherbet   And fancy thinking you weren't going to have a slice.

Foxtrot   You've got to have a slice.

Captain   I know, I know. But I've got a cupboard full of vitamins over there. It seems ludicrous to take them, then fill my stomach with –

Sherbet   It won't hurt you, Captain. Will it, Babe?

Foxtrot   Course not, Babe.

Sherbet   Not one slice.

Foxtrot   Not one slice.

Captain   But it does weaken one's defences and –

Sherbet   Fucking hell! Everyone wants to live for ever these days. And look younger. Vitamins for this. Plastic surgery for that. You wouldn't think immortality and eternal youth would be too much to ask for, would you? But it is! We all get old and drop dead some day. And all the fucking surgery and all the fucking tablets in the world won't help you one fucking atom.

Slight pause.

Cougar, I know what you're going through. Believe me. I do. Don't you think I know how guilty you feel about it all? Having a party like this when you so recently lost your wife. But she's gone, Cougar, and you've got to –

Foxtrot   Babe, I don't think you should –

Sherbet   No, Babe. This has to be said. There are certain things we have got to talk about tonight. That's why I'm here.

Foxtrot   But *I* asked you here.

Sherbet   Oh, Babe. Is that what you think? Bless.

Removes mask and hat.

I have a secret I want to tell. Something not even my Babe knows.

Foxtrot   What, Babe?

Sherbet   I need my handbag

Foxtrot *gets handbag and gives it to* **Sherbet**.

Slight pause.

Sherbet   One day, as I was walking up to the hospital to visit Babe's brother, I saw Babe leaving the hospital with a man. This man was wearing a leather jacket, white T-shirt, blue jeans, boots and his jet-black hair – his badly *dyed* jet-black hair – was styled in a quiff

Foxtrot   Babe, what're you –?

Sherbet   Shush, Babe.

Pause.

I mentioned this man to my Babe. Babe told me that this man was his new friend. He was called Cougar and he was in the hospital because his wife was dying. My Babe told me that Cougar was like a new older brother. And there were so many coincidences that linked them together. Ooo, I wanted to talk to this miraculous friend. Because that's what I thought it was. A miracle. But I was told I could not meet him. Why? Because meeting girls reminded him of his dying wife. I asked what the name of this dying wife was. Savannah Glass.

Slight pause.

One day I went to the hospital and my Babe's brother was dead.

Slight pause.

One day, two deaths.

Slight pause.

Because on that same day – probably at the very same minute for all I fucking know – your sister died. Is that right, Captain?

Captain   What? Oh . . . yes, yes.

Sherbet   Were you in the hospital?

Captain   I . . . I think so.

Sherbet   Don't you *know*?

Captain   Yes. I was.

Sherbet   Did she suffer?

Captain   No.

Sherbet   I'm so glad.

Pause.

One day, the day after I first heard about Savannah Glass, I asked a nurse where I could find her.

Captain   Good Lord!

Foxtrot   I told you not to!

Sherbet   I know, I know. But I felt I had to, you see.

Pause.

Sherbet   And the nurse took me to a ward. And . . . and this is my secret.

Pause.

I met Savannah Glass.

Captain *removes mask and hat.*

Captain   What's going on here?

Sherbet   I introduced myself.

Captain   What game are you playing?

Sherbet   What game am *I* playing?! That's a fucking fine one! Now, listen to me, Captain. I talked to Savannah for ages. She told me a lots and lots of things. What a wonderful creation she was. She told me one thing in particular. Something I have to mention now! Can you guess what it is?

Eh?

Slight pause.

Captain   What?

Sherbet   Cougar's real age.

Cougar *stands.*

Captain   For God's sake! Don't!

Foxtrot   Real age? But he's nineteen.

Sherbet   Don't be such a fucking idiot!

Foxtrot   I'm not a fucking idiot.

Sherbet   You don't know his type. I do! – I know your tricks, Cougar! Hear me? Knew them the first time I clocked you!

Captain   Stop it now!

Foxtrot   I don't understand.

Sherbet   I can guess your real age, Cougar!

Captain   Don't say it! Please. Don't say it.

Foxtrot   I don't care how old he is.

Sherbet   You hear me, Cougar?! I know your age.

Captain   For God's sake don't!

Cougar *starts to clutch his head and whine.*

Foxtrot   Your age don't matter. Honest.

Captain   Just go! Please! You don't know what you're doing!

Sherbet   I know exactly what I'm fucking doing!

Cougar *begins to whine louder. His sunglasses fall to the floor.*

Captain   Keep in control, Cougar.

Foxtrot   Just think about us. Our new start!

Cougar *steps towards* **Sherbet**, *the knife raised to strike.*

Captain   No!

Sherbet *takes a gun from her handbag and aims it at* **Cougar**.

Cougar *stops.*

Foxtrot   What the fuck're doing?!

Captain   Sherbet! Don't say it!

Sherbet   Shut up, both of you!

Pause.

Happy thirtieth birthday, Cougar.

Cougar *lets out a piercing howl. He hurls himself at* **Sherbet**, *knife raised.*

Foxtrot *lunges at* **Cougar**, *restraining the hand with the knife.*

Captain *rushes to* **Sherbet**, *grabbing the hand with gun.*

Aimed at the ceiling, the gun fires.

(All this happens in an instant!)

The moment the gun fires . . . all the lights (the sun-ray lamp included) start flickering violently, giving a strobe effect. And the birds start shrieking with deafening loudness. Everything exaggerated to the extreme.

Sherbet *is striking at* **Cougar**, **Cougar** *at her.*

Foxtrot *and* **Captain** *are trying to separate them.*

Foxtrot   Stop it, Cougar! Oh, God.

Captain   Don't! Don't! Let go of the gun! Let go before you kill someone.

Sherbet   Perhaps I want to fucking kill someone!

They are all fighting very violently now.

Sherbet *is striking at both* **Cougar** *and* **Captain**.

Cougar *is howling and trying to stab* **Sherbet** *with his knife.*

Foxtrot *begins to punch* **Cougar**. *Much kicking, hitting and clawing.*

Furniture gets knocked over, the tablecloth is pulled to the floor.

Sherbet *and* **Cougar** *are disarmed.*

Cougar *punches* **Sherbet** *repeatedly in the stomach.*

Sherbet *fights back, screams and kicks.*

Cougar *continues punching.*

Sherbet *bleeds profusely between legs.*

The blood goes everywhere

Foxtrot   Blood!

Sherbet   Ahhh! Blood! No! Blood!

Captain (*overlapping*)   Blood! Blood! Blood! Blood!

Sherbet (*overlapping*)   Blood! Blood! Blood! Blood!

Foxtrot (*overlapping*)   Blood! Blood! Blood! Blood!

Cougar *backs away from* **Sherbet** *and collapses to the floor, pulling curtains with him.*

At that precise moment the lights stop flickering and remain out.

Brilliant moonlight illuminates the room.

The shrieking birds remain, but their sound is diminishing.

Foxtrot *rushes to Sherbet.*

Foxtrot   Babe! Babe!

Captain *rushes to* **Sherbet**.

Captain   I'll get a towel.

Rushes to bathroom.

Foxtrot   Oh, Babe. Not the Future One. Not the Future –

Captain *rushes back with towel and puts it between* **Sherbet**'s *legs.*

Captain   Here! Sherbet! Sherbet!

Foxtrot *goes to* **Cougar**.

Foxtrot   What's fucking wrong with you? All I wanted to happen was . . . Fuck! Not this! I could fucking kill you, you crazy fuck! I could kill you!

Strikes **Cougar**.

Captain   Foxtrot, don't!

Foxtrot   Kill you! Kill you!

Captain *pulls* **Foxtrot** *off* **Cougar**.

Captain   There's no time for any of that! Just help me. Let's get Sherbet down to Cheetah Bee's. Quickly!

Foxtrot *and* **Captain** *carry* **Sherbet** *out of room and down corridor.*

Captain   Be careful!

Foxtrot   Oh, Babe!

Captain   Careful.

He knocks on **Cheetah**'s *door.*

Captain   Cheetah Bee! Emergency! Emergency!

Cheetah *opens door.*

Captain   We need an ambulance!

Cheetah   Sweet Jesus!

Captain   Hurry!

Captain *and* **Foxtrot** *carry* **Sherbet** *into* **Cheetah**'s *room. The door is closed behind them.*

Very long pause.

Slowly, **Cougar** *stands. He goes to mirror, takes comb from pocket and straightens his hair. When he's satisfied, he searches for his sunglasses and puts them on. He gives himself one last look in the mirror, then strolls round the room. He sees the remains of the birthday cake. He picks up the cake and sits at table. Slowly, he begins to eat cake.*

Long pause.

The door opens and **Captain** *enters.*

Captain *sees* **Cougar** *eating cake.*

Pause.

Captain *closes door behind him, then watches* **Cougar**.

Long pause.

Captain *sees gun on floor and picks it up.*

Cougar *continues to eat.*

Long pause.

A flashing light illuminates the window. It is the ambulance in the street below.

Captain *goes to window.*

Captain   The ambulance.

Cougar *doesn't react.*

Pause.

Captain   There's Foxtrot. He's crying. Sherbet's on a stretcher. She's crying too.

Pause.

The ambulance drives away.

Captain *turns to face* **Cougar**.

Cougar *continues to eat cake.*

Captain   She lost the baby.

Cougar *doesn't react.*

Pause.

Captain   Are you listening, Cougar? The baby's dead.

Cougar *doesn't react.*

Pause.

Slowly, **Captain** *aims the gun at* **Cougar**.

Cougar *is too engrossed in eating the cake to notice.*

Pause.

Captain *cocks the trigger. It makes a clicking sound.*

Still **Cougar** *doesn't look.*

Pause.

The door opens and **Cheetah** *appears.*

She sees **Captain** *holding gun.*

Captain *and* **Cheetah** *stare at each other.*

Captain *lowers the gun.*

Slowly, **Cheetah** *enters. She takes the gun from* **Captain** *and puts it in her coat pocket.*

She goes back to door, then look back at **Captain**.

Cheetah   One day, I went down to the factory to see how the animals were killed. I saw my husband take an animal from a cage. He held the animal by its back legs, then he swung it hard against the floor. The animal was stunned but it was not killed. Then my husband hung the animal from a metal hook and started to cut the fur from its body. He ripped the skin away as easily as peeling off a rubber glove. The animal struggled and screamed. There was no expression on my husband's face at all.

Cougar *has stopped eating the cake and is listening.*

Cheetah   Then my husband threw the skinned body into a metal container. I heard noises coming from inside the container. Tiny cries. I crept over and looked inside. I saw a mass of skinned bodies. All writhing. And their eyes. Sparkling dark eyes. Like black diamonds in red meat. All looking up at me . . . The cruelty of what I saw that day still chills me. But – oh . . .

Feels her fur coat.

It *is* beautiful.

Cheetah *exits, closing the door behind her.*

Pause.

Captain *looks out of window. He opens window and picks up dead bird from window sill.*

He takes bird over to table and sits opposite **Cougar**.

Pause.

Captain   And the Prince and the Blind Girl lived . . . happily together. And the years flew by them. Years became hours. Hours became seconds. Because The Fastest Clock in the Universe is . . .

Cougar   Love.

Captain   Hallelujah!

Fade to blackout.

Methuen Drama Student Editions

Jean Anouilh *Antigone* • John Arden *Serjeant Musgrave's Dance*
Alan Ayckbourn *Confusions* • Aphra Behn *The Rover* • Edward Bond
Lear • *Saved* • Bertolt Brecht *The Caucasian Chalk Circle* • *Fear and
Misery in the Third Reich* • *The Good Person of Szechwan* • *Life of Galileo* •
Mother Courage and her Children • *The Resistible Rise of Arturo Ui* • *The
Threepenny Opera* • Anton Chekhov *The Cherry Orchard* • *The Seagull* •
Three Sisters • *Uncle Vanya* • Caryl Churchill *Serious Money* • *Top Girls*
• Shelagh Delaney *A Taste of Honey* • Euripides *Elektra* • *Medea* •
Dario Fo *Accidental Death of an Anarchist* • Michael Frayn *Copenhagen*
• John Galsworthy *Strife* • Nikolai Gogol *The Government Inspector* •
Robert Holman *Across Oka* • Henrik Ibsen *A Doll's House* • *Ghosts* •
Hedda Gabler • Charlotte Keatley *My Mother Said I Never Should* •
Bernard Kops *Dreams of Anne Frank* • Federico García Lorca *Blood
Wedding* • *Doña Rosita the Spinster* (bilingual edition) • *The House of
Bernarda Alba* • (bilingual edition) • *Yerma* (bilingual edition) • David
Mamet *Glengarry Glen Ross* • *Oleanna* • Patrick Marber *Closer* • John
Marston *Malcontent* • Martin McDonagh *The Lieutenant of Inishmore* •
Joe Orton *Loot* • Luigi Pirandello *Six Characters in Search of an Author*
• Mark Ravenhill *Shopping and F***ing* • Willy Russell *Blood Brothers*
• *Educating Rita* • Sophocles *Antigone* • *Oedipus the King* • Wole
Soyinka *Death and the King's Horseman* • Shelagh Stephenson *The
Memory of Water* • August Strindberg *Miss Julie* • J. M. Synge *The
Playboy of the Western World* • Theatre Workshop *Oh What a Lovely
War* Timberlake Wertenbaker *Our Country's Good* • Arnold Wesker
The Merchant • Oscar Wilde *The Importance of Being Earnest* •
Tennessee Williams *A Streetcar Named Desire* • *The Glass Menagerie*

Methuen Drama Modern Plays
include work by

Edward Albee
Jean Anouilh
John Arden
Margaretta D'Arcy
Peter Barnes
Sebastian Barry
Brendan Behan
Dermot Bolger
Edward Bond
Bertolt Brecht
Howard Brenton
Anthony Burgess
Simon Burke
Jim Cartwright
Caryl Churchill
Noël Coward
Lucinda Coxon
Sarah Daniels
Nick Darke
Nick Dear
Shelagh Delaney
David Edgar
David Eldridge
Dario Fo
Michael Frayn
John Godber
Paul Godfrey
David Greig
John Guare
Peter Handke
David Harrower
Jonathan Harvey
Iain Heggie
Declan Hughes
Terry Johnson
Sarah Kane
Charlotte Keatley
Barrie Keeffe
Howard Korder

Robert Lepage
Doug Lucie
Martin McDonagh
John McGrath
Terrence McNally
David Mamet
Patrick Marber
Arthur Miller
Mtwa, Ngema & Simon
Tom Murphy
Phyllis Nagy
Peter Nichols
Sean O'Brien
Joseph O'Connor
Joe Orton
Louise Page
Joe Penhall
Luigi Pirandello
Stephen Poliakoff
Franca Rame
Mark Ravenhill
Philip Ridley
Reginald Rose
Willy Russell
Jean-Paul Sartre
Sam Shepard
Wole Soyinka
Simon Stephens
Shelagh Stephenson
Peter Straughan
C. P. Taylor
Theatre de Complicite
Theatre Workshop
Sue Townsend
Judy Upton
Timberlake Wertenbaker
Roy Williams
Snoo Wilson
Victoria Wood

Methuen Drama Contemporary Dramatists
include

John Arden (two volumes)
Arden & D'Arcy
Peter Barnes (three volumes)
Sebastian Barry
Dermot Bolger
Edward Bond (eight volumes)
Howard Brenton
  (two volumes)
Richard Cameron
Jim Cartwright
Caryl Churchill (two volumes)
Sarah Daniels (two volumes)
Nick Darke
David Edgar (three volumes)
David Eldridge
Ben Elton
Dario Fo (two volumes)
Michael Frayn (three volumes)
David Greig
John Godber (four volumes)
Paul Godfrey
John Guare
Lee Hall (two volumes)
Peter Handke
Jonathan Harvey
  (two volumes)
Declan Hughes
Terry Johnson (three volumes)
Sarah Kane
Barrie Keeffe
Bernard-Marie Koltès
  (two volumes)
Franz Xaver Kroetz
David Lan
Bryony Lavery
Deborah Levy
Doug Lucie

David Mamet (four volumes)
Martin McDonagh
Duncan McLean
Anthony Minghella
  (two volumes)
Tom Murphy (six volumes)
Phyllis Nagy
Anthony Neilsen (two volumes)
Philip Osment
Gary Owen
Louise Page
Stewart Parker (two volumes)
Joe Penhall (two volumes)
Stephen Poliakoff
  (three volumes)
David Rabe (two volumes)
Mark Ravenhill (two volumes)
Christina Reid
Philip Ridley
Willy Russell
Eric-Emmanuel Schmitt
Ntozake Shange
Sam Shepard (two volumes)
Wole Soyinka (two volumes)
Simon Stephens (two volumes)
Shelagh Stephenson
David Storey (three volumes)
Sue Townsend
Judy Upton
Michel Vinaver
  (two volumes)
Arnold Wesker (two volumes)
Michael Wilcox
Roy Williams (three volumes)
Snoo Wilson (two volumes)
David Wood (two volumes)
Victoria Wood

Methuen Drama World Classics

include

Jean Anouilh (two volumes)
Brendan Behan
Aphra Behn
Bertolt Brecht (eight volumes)
Büchner
Bulgakov
Calderón
Čapek
Anton Chekhov
Noël Coward (eight volumes)
Feydeau
Eduardo De Filippo
Max Frisch
John Galsworthy
Gogol
Gorky (two volumes)
Harley Granville Barker
  (two volumes)
Victor Hugo
Henrik Ibsen (six volumes)
Jarry

Lorca (three volumes)
Marivaux
Mustapha Matura
David Mercer (two volumes)
Arthur Miller (five volumes)
Molière
Musset
Peter Nichols (two volumes)
Joe Orton
A. W. Pinero
Luigi Pirandello
Terence Rattigan
  (two volumes)
W. Somerset Maugham
  (two volumes)
August Strindberg
  (three volumes)
J. M. Synge
Ramón del Valle-Inclan
Frank Wedekind
Oscar Wilde

Methuen Drama Classical Greek Dramatists

include

Aeschylus Plays: One
(Persians, Seven Against Thebes, Suppliants,
Prometheus Bound)

Aeschylus Plays: Two
(Oresteia: Agamemnon, Libation-Bearers, Eumenides)

Aristophanes Plays: One
(Acharnians, Knights, Peace, Lysistrata)

Aristophanes Plays: Two
(Wasps, Clouds, Birds, Festival Time, Frogs)

Aristophanes & Menander: New Comedy
(Women in Power, Wealth, The Malcontent,
The Woman from Samos)

Euripides Plays: One
(Medea, The Phoenician Women, Bacchae)

Euripides Plays: Two
(Hecuba, The Women of Troy,
Iphigeneia at Aulis, Cyclops)

Euripides Plays: Three
(Alkestis, Helen, Ion)

Euripides Plays: Four
(Elektra, Orestes, Iphigeneia in Tauris)

Euripides Plays: Five
(Andromache, Herakles' Children, Herakles)

Euripides Plays: Six
(Hippolytos, Suppliants, Rhesos)

Sophocles Plays: One
(Oedipus the King, Oedipus at Colonus, Antigone)

Sophocles Plays: Two
(Ajax, Women of Trachis, Electra, Philoctetes)

For a complete catalogue
of Methuen Drama titles
write to:

Methuen Drama
36 Soho Square
London W1D 3QY

or you can visit our website at:

www.methuendrama.com

Lightning Source UK Ltd.
Milton Keynes UK
UKOW03f2134091013

218752UK00007B/78/P